THE
BISCUIT

& TIMELY TALES BY
T. L. NEEDHAM

Outskirts Press, Inc.
http://www.outskirtspress.com

ISBN: 978-1-9772-2719-5

Cover Photo © 2020 T. L. Needham. All rights reserved - used with permission.

Outskirts Press and the "OP" logo are trademarks belonging to Outskirts Press, Inc.

PRINTED IN THE UNITED STATES OF AMERICA

"It is not more surprising to be born twice than once; everything in nature is resurrection."

—*Voltaire*

Dedicated to my father—Charles Vernon Needham II,
My grandfather—Charles Vernon Needham,
My great grandfather—Curtis Bayard Needham II,
And my great, great grandfather—Curtis Bayard Needham,
And all the fathers who came before them . . .

mem·oir*

/ˈmem‚wär/

noun

1. a historical account or biography written from personal knowledge or special sources.

Definition. **Memoirs** are factual stories about someone›s life. ‹**Memoir**› is from the French word mémoire, which means 'reminiscence' or 'memory.' They are a part of the nonfiction literary genre and are usually told in the first person.
[*source: google]

———=›‹‹◑››‹=———

Within is a collection of memoirs, in short stories, taken from my earliest childhood to adulthood. These stories are told to the best of my recollection, although some names, details, and places, are fictional composites; rendered to enhance the flow, yet remain true to the story.

———=›‹‹◑››‹=———

TABLE OF CONTENTS

I Do Believe . . .

Yes, I do believe in . . .
Angels, Reincarnation, and Karma.
I believe that birth and death
Are opposite sides of the same door.
And, I believe that love never dies,
But lives on forever,
And that you will meet those you love
Time and time again . . .
On both sides of that door.

—*T. L. Needham*

INTRODUCTION

A timely collection of short stories that starts with THE BISCUIT and ends with THE RING.

THE BISCUIT—A story about the times when you do the wrong thing, for the right reasons, and then the right thing, for the wrong reasons.

THE RING—It's not the kind you hear, but the kind you wear. A story about traveling with spirits in the car, not the kind you drink, but the other kind.

Within, is a collection of short stories about time, as in running out of time, wasting time as the meter keeps running, going back in time, as in dream time.

Plus, poems that, like a helium filled balloon, tug at the string you are holding, and, like your imagination, begs to be released to watch it fly away into the sky, until it vanishes, taking your dreams away with it.

So, what about time? Well, it is funny stuff. We are born into this world with nothing, but time. And, we never know how much time we have, until we run out of time and leave this world. Then we are left with nothing, but the memories.

So, my advice is, take your time. Spend your time wisely, never waste time, and always make time . . . for those you love.

"I know I am deathless. No doubt I have died myself ten thousand times before. I laugh at what you call dissolution, and I know the amplitude of time."
—Walt Whitman

THE BISCUIT

"DAD TAKE A look at this," I said, pulling my fist from my pocket closed around an object and extending the closed hand toward him.

He held up his hand with a look of wary curiosity on his face, while sitting in his creaky old rocking chair. Holding my out-stretched hand out over his wrinkled old hand, palm turned up, I laid the contents of my closed fist upon his hand.

A slight smile curled the corner of his mouth, and I saw a little twinkle of light in his eyes as he beheld a gleaming and hefty pocket watch sitting in his open palm.

"A biscuit . . ." Dad said, as he cradled the watch in his hand with tender regard, as if he were holding something alive. "Where did you get this?" he asked, without taking his eyes off the lovely thing. Dad had to retire early when he was about sixty, due to a heart condition, just after Mom passed away. Since then he was frail and sad all too often.

"Well, Dad, I have wanted a pocket watch since that job in-terview with Alexander Proudfoot of Chicago about ten years ago. The man conducting the interview had the most beautiful pocket watch I had ever seen. When I admired it, he went on to describe how much he loved pocket watches and collecting them. He said that thanks to his high income, he could afford to buy any watch he wanted, and, since he had no family, but only himself to spend his money on, he could easily afford this expensive hobby."

Dad said nothing, now carefully examining the pocket watch I had placed in his shaky hand. So, I continued my explanation of this new acquisition.

"Well, you know Frances, my mother-in-law, recently inherited the entire estate from a woman she had taken care of for many years, who passed away recently. This pocket watch was one of the many things included in the estate. It had belonged to this woman's father, who passed away back in the early 1930s. I was admiring the watch so much that Frances just gave it to me. Can you imagine that? I was thrilled!"

"Do you mind if I take a look inside?" Dad asked, as he looked up at me for the first time since I laid the watch in his hand.

"Sure Dad, but tell me, why did you call this watch a 'biscuit' a moment ago?"

I had no idea how to open the watch to look inside so I was amazed when Dad pressed the watch between the palms of his weathered and veined old hands, then winced as he gave the watch a firm, yet careful, twist. The back screwed off and Dad set it on the table beside him. Then, as he studied the inside of the watch with a magnifying glass he kept nearby to help him read fine print, he said, "That is what we called them on the railroad . . . 'Biscuit' . . . cause a pocket watch is about the same size as a standard biscuit."

After a few quiet moments, as Dad carefully examined the interior of the watch, he finally said, "Son, this is an excellent watch. It is a 23-jewel, Waltham Vanguard railroad watch."

"What makes a 'railroad watch' so special Dad?" I asked, eager to know more about my new watch, especially if it was something that added value to my recent acquisition. Dad had been a life-long employee of the Union Pacific Railroad, so he knew everything about railroading, including watches. Yet, I had never known Dad to own a pocket watch himself.

"Keeping accurate time was critical on the railroad, son. It was not just about being sure the trains ran on time either. It was a matter of life or death. A terrible train wreck that took many lives happened way back in the early 1890s, because the engineer's watch had stopped, then started again, but was just a few minutes slow. After that, railroads established strict rules and standards for time keeping by all employees. They required all employees involved in train movement to own a watch, and it had to be an approved 'railroad' watch . . . one that met the certain standards set by the railroad. For example, one requirement was the lever setting, which required that a watch could be wound without accidentally altering the time setting. The railroad watch was made to specifications required by the railroad, including the number of jewels, plus the number of adjustments."

"Adjustments? What do you mean Dad? Other than keeping good time, what else matters for a watch?" I asked.

"Adjustments meant the watch had to be specially calibrated to keep accurate time regardless of the position it is held, so it would work in the vertical or horizontal, the left or right, or upside down position. Railroad work could get pretty rough you know," as Dad continued to talk, all the while his eyes never looked up from examining the inside of the watch.

Finally, Dad looked up from the watch, and, looking straight into my eyes, said, "Son, this is a really fine watch. Not a fancy watch, but a fine workingman's watch. It has a silver-nickel case, 23-jewel movement, and it looks like it is all here."

I said nothing as I watched my Dad slowly screw the cover of the watch back into place. He was very quiet too. Then Dad looked up at me again, and as our eyes met, I noticed a redness as moisture welled up within his eyes, when he asked, "Son, would you sell this watch to me?"

I was shocked by this question and I did not expect it. Yet, I could clearly see in my Dad's eyes that he really wanted this watch. I instantly realized that for the first time in my life, I actually owned something my Dad wanted. So ironic for me to fully grasp . . . I mean, Dad was there for me all my life and he always provided for my needs. However, he always lived a simple life and had all he needed because he wanted so little. In fact, nothing was harder than trying to come up with any gift ideas for Dad on his birthdays . . . except maybe a custard pie from his favorite diner.

But here he was, clearly wanting . . . no, desperately seeking . . . to own something that I possessed. Then I also remembered that this watch was a gift to me from someone who could have given it to her own husband, who was also a retired railroad man, or to one of her two grandsons. But no, she gave it to me because she knew I really wanted it; had always wanted a good pocket watch; and she was showing me an act of great kindness and generosity. How would it look if, after that, I just turned around and sold the watch for a few bucks? I found myself in a real dilemma.

Then, after a long and awkward silence between my Dad and myself, as he sat there staring at the lovely Waltham railroad watch cradled in the palm of his hand as if it were alive, and he did not want to smother it, but, only comfort it, I said, "Dad, I cannot sell you that watch. It was a gift to me. It just would not be right. But I can loan it to you, to keep for me for the rest of your life. Just be certain I get it back when you are done with it—deal?"

Dad did not look up. His eyes continued to gaze down upon the watch. But, after a long moment, I saw his head begin to slowly rise up and down to nod in agreement. Then he finally looked up, still with red-wet eyes, and with a wide grin on his face, as he said, "Deal, son."

As Dad slipped the 'biscuit-watch' into the bib pocket of his overalls, he said, "You know I never felt I could afford to buy a watch like this while I worked for the railroad, even though they would sell one to me on a $1.00 a week plan, deducted from each paycheck. I never felt it was right to buy anything on 'time' payments. Cash only for me; if you could not pay for it now, you could not afford it. I just never believed in spending money I did not have."

"But, my Pa, your old granddad, did have an old 'Father-Time' railroad watch made by Elgin," Dad continued. "Yes, my old man worked for the same railroad his entire life and told me he would give me a lickin' if he ever saw me working down there too. But when I got married and you kids started coming, well, that was just the best work I could get, and he understood. Yet, when my Pa died at the age of 82-years, back in '72, well, Ma went and gave Pa's watch to Clarence, my younger brother. She knew I wanted it too. Plus, being the oldest son, I think I should have gotten it, but that was Ma's way of doing things."

After sitting quietly for a few moments in his big old rocking chair, reflecting on his thoughts of his father's watch, my Dad said, "I actually had quite a few of these railroad watches in my possession over the years. Could have kept a few too, I guess. You see, son, times were always very tough back in the late '30s and during World War II, so many of my co-workers would come up short of cash between paychecks. But I was always very careful with my money and never let myself go broke. I always had some pocket money. So, those who did go broke would come to me and ask, 'Vern, could you loan me $5 until next payday? I will let you keep my railroad watch as collateral."

"There were times when I had a dozen or so watches in my locker. Most fellas always paid me back. But there were a few who never did, or could; yet, I never kept a man's watch. Eventually, I would just return it to them, loan paid back or not. But there was one time when I was given a watch by a young fella in return for a favor, I did for him."

"It was on a day when I got to work at the rail yards and was walking across the tracks between the freight cars on my way to my job in the round house. I was a welder-carman back then, which meant I fixed broken things on any railroad rolling stock. As I stepped across the tracks between two trains, I heard a commotion. I turned my head down the track and could see a railroad detective, or 'Bull' as we called them, dragging a hobo out of an open boxcar door. He slammed the hapless man to the ground and began to beat him with his blackjack. The thick leather bludgeon with the lead weight inside was doing some real damage to the old tramp, and he soon appeared to be unconscious. Yet, the Bull just kept punishing him with repeated blows. He did not see me walking up behind him. I grabbed the blackjack out of his hand as he swung back for another blow. Then I spun the surprised Bull around and said, 'I think he has had enough . . . don't you?' We were eye-to-eye, and he was furious at me for my interference in the beating. But he must have seen something just as serious in my eyes because he calmed down instantly and quietly said, 'Guess maybe you are right,' and he held out his hand for me to return his blackjack. I stepped back a few strides to put space between us, and I said, 'Maybe I should just keep this,' while hefting the blackjack in my hand a time or two."

"There will be hell to pay if you do!" he said. So, after a couple more steps backwards, I tossed the blackjack back to him and turned to continue my walk to the round house, and I thought to myself, 'Damn Pussyfoot!'"

"Turns out that old Bull, or Pussyfoot, as we called them—because they were always sneaking around and spying on us workers—had decided to keep an eye on me the rest of the day. Later that morning, I was working on something for myself on my lunch break. It was a trailer hitch for my truck. The Pussyfoot sneaked up on me when I was not looking and asked me what I was working on. I said, '. . . door closer . . .' We were always having trouble closing stuck doors on box cars, so this seemed to make sense to him. He said, 'Well, here let me help you,' and he held the long end of a steel bar I was cutting with my hacksaw. I just kept working and ignored him. But he was definitely making me nervous. I could see he was still spying on me.

"Not long after the Pussyfoot left, a young fella named Huey walked into the round house. I was holding his railroad watch for a loan that was long overdue, so I expected he was here to pay up and retrieve his watch. Instead, he said, 'Vern, I need a favor. When I was driving to work this morning, I hit a deep pothole and it looks like it broke my tie-rod. So, I can't steer my car very well. I know I owe you money, and now I am really in a fix, cause my gal and I were going to drive down to Miami, Oklahoma tomorrow and get married. But I could never make it now with that broken tie-rod. Think you could help me out Vern? If you could do this for me, you can keep my railroad watch. It's worth much more than what I owe you.'"

Dad paused in his story telling for a moment to catch his breath and to take a long gulp on his coffee he kept sitting next to him. Then, as he continued, I could visualize the events in my mind as he described them:

Vern checked his wristwatch. He still had some time left on his lunch hour. Then he stepped outside the round house to look around and see if that Pussyfoot was still lurking in the area. Knowing he could get fired for doing personal work on railroad property, Vern turned to Huey and said, "Okay, I can get your car going again, but you better make yourself scarce for now."

"Thanks! I will come back later at the end of my shift to pick up my car," Huey said, as he tossed the car keys to Vern.

Within just a few minutes, Vern had used the heavy-lift hoist to raise the front end of the car into the air so high that he could work on the broken tie-rod while standing up. He had clamped the two broken pieces together, put on his welder's mask and was in the process of making the final weld when someone tapped him on the back of his shoulder. Vern could not stop in the middle of the weld-pass without ruining the weld, so he just kept his mask down and continued welding. He got tapped again on the back of his shoulder, more insistently this time. Finally, the weld-pass was done, and Vern threw back his welder's mask as he turned to see who was bothering him while he was busy making a weld. There was the Pussyfoot-Bull, standing right behind him.

"Just what are you doing to that car?" the Bull demanded.

"What the hell does it look like?" Vern responded, standing nose-to-nose to the man, once again.

"Is that your car you are working on?"

"No."

"Well, who the hell does it belong to?" the Bull shouted in Vern's face.

"That is between me and him—and I am not telling YOU!" Vern shouted back to the Bull, emphatically, and in no uncertain terms—pointing his finger at the Bull's nose.

Vern realized at this point that he had nothing left to lose. He had been caught red-handed by a railroad detective working on personal property while on railroad property. This was cause for instant termination, but he also knew they would fire young Huey too. So, while Vern was fighting the urge to punch the Pussyfoot in the nose—to add that to the reasons he would be fired—the Pussyfoot pointed his finger right at Vern's nose and said, "You can clean out your locker, and I am going to find your foreman!"

It took a while for Vern to put away his welder gear and walk back to the locker room. By the time he got there, his foreman,

Hutch, had already heard the news and was waiting for him. When Vern saw Hutch, he realized he had also gotten him into a lot of trouble in this incident too.

"I am so sorry Hutch," Vern said, as he opened his locker and reached inside to retrieve Huey's railroad watch. "Please give this to Huey and his car keys too. Tell him I wish him luck, and that I never told the Bull it was his car. So, he better get it out of here as fast as he can. He is most likely still 'pussyfooting' around here."

Just then, Huey walked into the locker room too. "Vern, I heard what happened! I am so sorry I got you in trouble!"

Hutch, who had still not spoken, handed the keys and the pocket watch to Huey, saying, "Here, I think these belong to you?"

Huey took the car keys and pocket watch. Then he handed the pocket watch back to Vern and said, "Vern, this is yours now, you have more than earned it . . . and a deal is a deal."

Vern looked at the pocket watch. In his mind, he was no longer going to be working for the railroad, at least not THIS railroad. He had less use for a pocket watch now; plus, he knew Huey was a switchman, and owning a pocket watch was required for his work. "You keep this, Huey," Vern said. "Wedding present." Vern smiled, extended his hand to shake Huey's hand, saying, "Congratulations to you and your sweetheart."

Huey was speechless, and, feeling a little choked up, chose to say nothing and just walked out of the locker room with his railroad pocket watch in his pocket.

Hutch finally spoke up, "Vern, you sure can make a mess for me, like no one I have ever known. I cannot imagine how someone can get caught doing the right thing, at the wrong time, for the right reasons, but with the wrong outcome!"

"Well, Hutch, you just have to play the hand you are dealt, and today I drew a losing hand," Vern said, as he turned to finish clearing out his locker.

"Well, we will see about that," Hutch said, "But stop cleaning out your locker. You're not fired and not going anywhere. I'm transferring you to the wrecker crew where you'll be on-the-road most of the time. Maybe that way you can stay out of trouble around here. Good men like you are hard to find, and we cannot afford to lose you."

"What about that Bull?" Vern asked.

"Do not worry about him. He's from headquarters in Omaha. Not one of the local boys. He'll file his report. But, by the time it gets back here—it may all just blow over. So, just let me worry about that," Hutch replied with a wink and a big grin on his face.

"Hutch was a good man," Dad said, as he finished his story. "So, that is the closest I ever came to own a real railroad pocket watch, son—until today"

Thirty-two years later, after driving all night to get back home to see Dad, who was in the hospital, I found myself remembering that evening as if it were only yesterday. I recalled the countless times I had seen Dad over those many years when I would ask him, "Say, Dad, what time is it?" Just to give him the excuse to pull that old "biscuit" out of the bib pocket of his overalls and check the time. But, sadly, now Dad was running out of time. He was 92-years old and had carried the "biscuit" for over 32-years, just over one-third of his life. A hospice worker was sitting in Dad's darkened room.

She stood to greet me when I arrived.

"He is very weak and very quiet right now, but his time is short; he may leave us any minute now," she said. Then she walked out of the room, leaving me alone with Dad. After a few quiet moments, Dad woke up. His eyes were barely opened. He smiled to see me in his room. Dad seemed a little dazed, like he was not sure if he was dreaming, as he asked if it was really me? Just then, a nurse stepped in and saw that he was awake. She asked if he was hungry—Dad was always hungry—but he did not respond.

"I have a cup of strawberry ice cream?" She offered, with the smile of an angel.

Dad nodded his head slightly, with a hint of a smile.

"That is his favorite," I said as she handed me the tiny cup of ice cream and a spoon.

So, I spent the remaining minutes with Dad, feeding him his favorite dish of strawberry ice cream. To make conversation, I asked Dad what's the secret to his very long life? He said, "Well son, I just never worried about anything I could do nothing about. And, I could not do anything about nearly everything!" Even near his end, Dad was making jokes. Then we sat quietly, Dad in bed with labored breaths, and me in the chair on his right. I was holding his right hand while I quietly said the Rosary. Then, his left hand rose up—as if he was reaching for something, or someone. As his left arm slowly fell back down to the bed, Dad took his last breath. He then passed quietly; and still had that same slight smile.

A little while later I was going through Dad's things in his clothing. There I found the old "biscuit" on a watch fob just inside the bib pocket in his overalls; right where he always kept it. I had let him keep the fine old "biscuit" until he was done with it, just as we had agreed so many years ago. Now it meant so much more to me than it ever could have otherwise.

Dad is gone now. Now, there is just the biscuit, the memories, and me. He gave back to me the same joy I had given him in that ordinary timepiece of extraordinary significance. Dad lived a long life . . . 92-years. He outlived his Ma and his Pa, his three younger brothers, his beloved wife, and all of her family too. He passed on without regret or fear, for he knew he used his time here as well as he could— "Always playing the hand he was dealt." And, he knew that where he was going—he would never be lonely. In doing so, Dad gave me the best gift of all . . . the memories.

My Dad, Charles Vernon
Needham, Jr. "Vern"

The Old Swing

Memories of warm summer days,
Seeking shade on the old swing
Under the arbor covered with
Grape vines, faded too soon,
As autumn's chill arrived.

—T. L. Needham

REDEMPTION
IN DAD'S EYES

ONCE DAD ACCIDENTALLY locked us all out of the house. Dad got pretty mad on those occasions, even at himself. He stomped around the house and found all the doors and windows were locked, except a small window in the kitchen. But it was too small for anyone to fit through, except little two-year old me.

So, Dad pushed the window open as wide as it would go. Then he picked me up and stuck me feet first through the window. There was an old nail, bent over, on the windowsill forming a hook to latch the screen. I sliced my butt on that old nail as Dad slid me over the sill. I let out a yelp and dropped to the floor. Then Dad ran around to the back-kitchen door and started yelling instructions to me through the glass to unlock the back door. I limped over to the back door, holding my wounded bottom in one hand, as I whined for sympathy.

I was not strong enough to turn the latchkey and unlock the door from the inside. I tried my best, but just could not do it. In frustration, Dad turned his back and shoved his elbow though the window . . . breaking the glass . . . so he could reach inside and unlatch the lock. I felt like such a useless wimp.

But I did get some redemption in Dad's eyes when my little

sister Patty was born. Mom was in the hospital giving birth to Patty, our newest family member. It was just after New Year's Day and my brother Charlie and sister Sue were back in school. I was only two and a half years old, so Dad left me at Grandma and Grandpa's home to baby-sit me. When Dad got off work in the evening, he arrived to pick me up and we stayed for dinner.

The weather was frigid, and an icy snowstorm had blanketed the city over New Years. When we left my grandparent's home, Dad had me sitting in front with him, a rare treat for me. After Dad backed down the driveway and put the car in gear to move forward, the car would not move.

Dad had set the emergency brake when he parked in his parent's driveway. Now the wet, slushy snow had frozen the brake cable in lock position, and it would not release. Dad began to swear under his breath as he got out, retrieved a ball-peen hammer from the toolbox he kept in the trunk, and crawled under the car. I could hear him banging on the frozen brake cable, and swearing as he lay in the icy, slushy road. The car was sitting on a slight hill so as soon as the brake released from Dad's hammering—the car began to roll forward while Dad was still lying underneath!

I realized, even at my very young age, that Dad was going to be pinned under the car as it rolled forward. Instantly I slid across the seat to get behind the steering wheel. I looked down and saw three pedals on the floor. I knew one made the car go, the other made it stop and had no idea what the third pedal did, but I knew I had to stop the rolling car now . . . or Dad would be pinned under the tire. I decided to push down on the middle pedal, which proved to be the right choice, but I could not reach the pedal while sitting on the seat. I was too small. So, I slid off the seat, placed both feet on the middle pedal and pushed, while I hung onto the steering wheel with both hands, and all my strength . . . hanging there, rigid under the steering wheel. It worked; the car stopped. I heard Dad shuffle out from under the car.

As Dad stood up and opened the driver side door, he saw me hanging under the steering wheel, holding on tight with both hands, as both my feet pressed on the middle pedal. I saw a blended look of surprise and rare approval in my Dad's eyes, and a slight smile on his face. That event helped me learn that you never know when someone's time may be up, unless you do all that you can do, to make a difference.

It Is . . .

I know something,
And it is wonderful.
You should know it too.
I want to tell you about it,
But it is best that you
Discover it for yourself.
So, all I can say is . . .
Never stop searching for it,
Because something wonderful
Is waiting for you . . .
To discover what it is.

—*T. L. Needham*

THE OLD FAUCET

Terry, this is your grandpa. I need your help. Please. I want you to drive me to the Kansas City Star office, right now. Why Grandpa? Because I need to get tomorrow's newspaper today. I am in my car right now, parked in front of your house, but you need to drive, because I am too old to deal with city traffic. I looked out the window as I hung up the phone. There was my Grandpa sitting on the passenger side of his black 1953 Ford, parked in front of my house. I rushed outside, got behind the wheel, put the car in gear and we sped off towards downtown and the office of the Kansas City Star, in a frantic rush!

I WOKE UP in a cold sweat. A glance at the clock showed I had overslept and needed to rush to make it to the office in time. But, the dream about my grandpa buzzed around in my mind. I laughed to myself, asking why would Grandpa need to get "tomorrows" newspaper—today? Clearly, it is today, and tomorrow's paper is not available until tomorrow.

Then I reminded myself of the time, when I was just a boy, that I asked my grandpa, "Hey Grandpa, what time is it?"

And, he replied without hesitation, "Hell, I don't know . . . for all I know it might be tomorrow."

So, why would it be unusual for him to want tomorrow's paper today? Then I realized, wait a minute, I never have dreamed about my Grandpa before. Not once in my life that I could recall. This is different. He is reaching out to me. I seldom even visit my grandpa unless there are other relatives in town and the family gathers at Grandma and Grandpa's place for a meal. In fact, as a rush of guilt swept over me, I have not once visited my grandpa in my adulthood . . . just to go see him. Not once. Sure, I had been busy working my way through college while I worked full-time at General Motors. So, that settles it. I am going to visit my Grandpa today.

I called my office to tell them I would be taking the day off. I finished getting dressed, grabbed a quick cup of coffee, and glanced at the newspaper. I did not want to show up at Grandpa's having not read the paper. That was something he and my Dad always did; they read the newspaper, every word, every day. Therefore, there was always something, no, a lot to talk about.

As I drove myself across town to Grandma and Grandpa's home, I found myself recalling my earliest memories of him. I was only two years old, but I remember this clearly. I was wearing my favorite blue T-shirt with an image of a Teddy Bear dipping his paw into a honey pot. He was a very happy Teddy Bear, and I loved him, and this shirt, and honey!

Well, my family arrived for a visit on a day when Grandpa had been painting a chair. As we arrived, he set the paint aside to greet us, with the wet paint brush sitting across the open paint can. As everyone greeted each other, I was instantly drawn to the wet brush and paint can.

Perhaps it was the color, a chocolate brown, that I found irre- sistible. Whatever, within a moment, I had chocolate brown paint on my mouth, face, both hands, my arms, and my favorite blue T-Shirt. Grandma noticed me first and yelled out, "Oh no! Look what you have gotten into . . . that will never clean off!"

I caught my mother's eyes next as she turned and saw my paint covered self, as a look of shock replaced her usual happy smile. But it was Grandpa who instantly came to my rescue. "This is all my fault," he said. "I never should have left the paint where he could get to it."

Feeling suddenly threatened and ashamed of my bad behavior, I expected a whipping was eminent. However, to my pleasant surprise, my Grandpa picked me up and carried me into his garage. I had never been inside his garage. It had a dirt floor that was soaked over the years with leaking motor old, transmission fluid, grease, and whatever. The odor was uniquely chemical, but in a pleasant way, and I never forgot it.

The walls and ceiling were covered with cobwebs and an array of old-timey looking stuff hanging haphazardly. And, it was dimly lit with only two dust covered windows on the south side admitting light.

Grandpa set me down on his workbench, in front of the double windows. He mumbled to me, "Do not worry sonny, we can clean this off." He opened a can of turpentine and soaked a shop rag with it. As he began to wipe my face, and arms and hands, after pulling off my blue T-shirt, I was nearly overcome by the vapors of that turpentine. Grandpa sensed this, so he reached behind me to open the windows over the workbench to let in a breeze of fresh air. Then I looked in his eyes . . . and saw the amused twinkle of absolute love and kindness. Something in that moment touched my heart, forever. In an unforgettable instant, I realized what a gentle and loving soul my Grandpa was; and how much he loved me too.

I arrived at Grandpa's gravel driveway, just in time to see him bending over to pick up his morning newspaper; a daily ritual for him, to start each day. He looked up and did not recognize my car, since I was such a rare visitor. I lowered my window and yelled out, "Hello you old faucet," a traditional greeting, I had heard my own Dad use every time he greeted his father on our visits. Grandpa recognized my face and smiled, as he stepped over to my car. "Hello stranger, are you lost?" he asked, with a wide grin on his face that squeezed out a little tobacco juice from the chew he always had stuffed in his cheek. That was Grandpa, always ready with a joke on a moment's notice. So, I rebutted . . . "Not lost old-timer, just looking for a handout!"

"Well, come on in and we'll see what's cooking." Grandpa said, with a wave of his hand up the driveway, as he turned his back, and started his walk back to the house.

"Grandpa, just how did you get the nickname— 'old faucet' that I have heard my Dad call you all my life?" I asked, as we shook hands. Grandpa measured the strength of my grip, again, with that amused twinkle in his eye.

As he released my hand from his iron-vise grip, he turned to walk up the steps to his front porch and into the house. "Well, sonny, it started before you were born. We have to thank your older brother, Charlie the 3rd, for that one. You see, your Dad would always greet me as, 'Hello, you old fossil!' But, young Charlie, when he was only about two, had no idea what a fossil was, so he would repeat his Dad's greeting by saying, 'Hello you old FAUCET!'"

Grandpa's shoulders shook a little with laugher, as a smile crossed his face at this happy memory.

We walked into the kitchen, as Grandma was cooking bacon and eggs in a half-inch deep puddle of bacon grease in an iron skillet on the stove. Smelled like heaven to me. "Hello Grandma!"

"Take a seat and pour yourself a coffee and one for Pa too," Grandma said. She was never much on affectionate greetings, no big hello hugs around here, just don't cross her and all was fine.

Grandpa's smile faded a little then too, as he sat down in his ancient chair at the head of the table. I poured each of us a cup of coffee. Grandpa's coffee cup was an old white mug, with thick sides and an extra big handle. He had made his own knife, fork and spoon, with extra-large wooden handles to enable him to get a good grip on them.

I recalled that nearly twenty years ago, he had both his hands crushed in an accident on the railroad. Grandpa worked as a car-man, which meant he fixed whatever broke on a railroad car. Well, once he was changing bearings in a wheel housing and the car weight was being held off the axle by a big crane. But, the crane-hold slipped and suddenly dropped the weight of the car onto the wheel housing, catching his hands. He was wearing heavy leather work gloves, which help give some protection as he pulled his left hand free, but the fingers in his right hand were crushed. I recall he had a full hand cast on, with what looked like finishing nails sticking out of the cast. They were used to pin and hold the fragments of his finger bones together until they healed. This left Grandpa with a weakened grip on his left hand, and he could barely close his right hand, but still had a good grip, up to a point. He could barely grip anything smaller than the size of a broom handle with his right hand. So, his coffee cup and eating utensils all had big, thick handles for him to grip.

Grandpa was also left with palsy in both hands, especially his injured right hand. Those involuntary tremors made his hands really shake and quiver whenever he picked up anything. Such as when he took his coffee cup in both hands, to try to steady it, as he raised it to his lips. The cup would shake, and the coffee would slosh out and up on one side then the other, and always fell right back into the cup. The shaking and sloshing continued until the cup reached his mouth, then it steadied just long enough for Grandpa to slurp his coffee. He never spilled a drop.

Watching this reminded me of a time when Grandpa's shaky hand and poor grip nearly took my head off. Grandpa was retired early by the railroad because of his injured hands. So, the first thing he did was get busy building on a bathroom to his home. He had built his home himself, along with his dad, my great grandpa Curtis. But it never included an indoor bathroom. The outhouse was in back, behind the garage, and baths were taken in a big washtub on the kitchen floor.

On the day Grandpa was finishing the roofing on his new bathroom addition I had been kept home from school due to illness. Mom and Dad both worked, and I was only 10-years old and too young to be left home alone. So, they left me at Grandma and Grandpa's house. It was fascinating to stand in the back yard and watch Grandpa up on the roof hammering roofing nails into those shingles. As he raised his hammer each time, to drive down a nail, he would glance back at me. I had no idea why Grandpa kept looking back at me.

Then Grandpa stopped hammering, put his hammer down, and backed off the roof, then down the ladder. At the bottom of the ladder, he turned his gaze toward me. I felt I was in trouble. I had no idea what I had done to suddenly merit his attention. He walked right up to me, towering over me in his bibbed coveralls, he looked down into my eyes and again, I saw that familiar kindness in his deep set, yet, "twinkle with joy" eyes. He put a hand on each of my shoulders and gently pushed me aside about ten paces off to the right.

"You stay right here now Sonny, and do not move. Okay?"

"Yes Grandpa."

He turned his back, walked back over to the ladder and climbed back up onto the roof. I watched as he picked a roofing nail from his apron and picked up his hammer in his right hand. Then, he tapped the nail to set it, and swung back his arm with full force to drive that hammer to the nail. But the hammer flew out of his hand! It went spinning back with full force right over the spot where I had been standing! If Grandpa had not moved me, I would certainly have been hit right in the head.

What made this moment so memorable was the thoughtful and gentle kindness of my Grandpa. He did not look back and see that I might be in the line-of-fire if he lost his grip on the hammer, and yell at me to move, or go away. No. He took the time and effort to stop what he was doing, put down his hammer, interrupt his work, and climb down that ladder and with gentle kindness, move me out of harm's way. That was my Grandpa.

Grandma asked us to move out of the kitchen because she need-ed the table clear to make lunch. So, Grandpa and I moved into the living room. Grandpa sat in his old oak-rocker, near the coal-burn-ing monkey stove. He put a fresh bite of tobacco chaw in his cheek and worked it with a few chews. Then he spit tobacco-juice in the big Folgers Coffee gallon can sitting on the floor, on a newspaper, to catch the missed spit and splatters.

I pulled a chair up right beside my Grandpa, anxious to chew on more memories. "Grandpa, my Dad told me you once had a run-in with the KKK and actually had a cross burned in the front yard. What happened?"

Grandpa got a distant, misty look in his eyes, as he let his mind work to recall that event decades ago. He worked his chaw a couple of times and took a spit in the can.

"Well, sonny, it was a very long time ago. A major snowstorm came in and covered the town with a thick blanket of snow. It stopped everything. But I had an old Corliss truck, with tandem rear wheels. I had a set of chains on both sides to get traction, so I had no trouble getting around.

But, the old Strang car line, which ran just north of my house, from Olathe to downtown Kansas City, was not running. As I pulled out of my driveway, I could see someone walking along the Strang tracks. It was brutally cold and windy. A hellish time for anyone to be walking outside. So, I pulled up alongside the tracks and opened my window. The person walking had his head down and leaned into the wind. I had to yell, to asked if he might need a ride? As he lifted his head to reply, I could see he was an older black man. He had already walked several miles in a determined effort to make it to work. He smiled broadly, revealing a gleaming mouth of white teeth."

"Sure, you betcha!" He said as he scampered in the deep snow off the tracks and around to the passenger door of my truck. I asked him where he was headed, and he said he worked for the Union Pacific, same railroad as me. He was a porter at the train station and had never missed a day of work. I worked in the yards near the station, so it was right on my way.

As I drove through the yards to drop my rider off behind the Union Station, several of my co-workers saw my passenger and me. Later that day, a couple of them approached and asked what the hell I was doing giving a ride to a black man? Well, I never cared for these fellas, or their attitude about a lot of things. So, I told them it was none of their business. Then, at the end of the shift, I made a point to wait for my black rider to get off work and walk out the back of the station. I offered him a ride home as far as my own house. He gladly accepted.

That night, around midnight, I heard a commotion out in the front yard. There it was, a big flaming cross burning like a gasoline fire. In the light of the flame I saw two men rush off and get into a car and drive away.

"What did you do next Grandpa?" I asked, alarmed that he and Grandma were in danger.

"Well, Sonny, the next morning, I got up early and drove my truck down the Strang line tracks away from town, until I saw my rider from the day before. I warned him about the threats I had been given and asked him if he would like another ride."

I saw a delightful twinkle of defiance in my Grandpa's eyes; as a smile curled the corners of his mouth, squeezing out a little tobacco juice.

"That old black porter and I became good friends and I often gave him a ride after that, if the Strang line was down. No one ever said another word about it to me either."

Grandpa and I continued to talk until lunchtime. Grandma had kept busy in the kitchen and never said a word to us. But, in their tiny cottage, she could hear every word. We were both glad to hear her finally say, "If you're hungry you better get to the table before I throw it out."

Grandma always kept a feisty edge on her tongue, but she meant well. So, Grandpa and I wasted no time moving to the kitchen table. There, in the middle, was a steaming bowl of chicken and dumplings. Those dumplings Grandma made were always light as a cloud and soft as an angel food cake-biscuit. The only thing that kept them floating away was that thick layer of golden chicken gravy they rested on. The talk took a break while we all enjoyed this wonderful meal.

After lunch, Grandpa and I resumed our chat, back in the living room. I asked him why he called my Dad Vern?

Grampa explained that my Dad was a junior, since he was given the same name as his, Charles Vernon Needham. And, when they ended up both working for the Union Pacific railroad, and he was already called "Charlie" by everyone, well, your Dad needed a different name, so it became "Vern" . . . to our co-workers on the railroad.

Next, I asked Grandpa if he remembered locking up my Dad's car? He got that misty look in his eyes as he took himself back in time and replied, "Your Dad was like most youngsters when he got old enough to drive. Full of fun, and low on good sense. So, I set a curfew for him of midnight to get home every evening, or, he would be locked out. Just not much to do after midnight but get into some kind of orneriness. So, sure enough, that very night after I set the curfew, he got home after midnight. I did not lock him out. It was raining as I recall. So, the next morning, I just took a heavy logging chain and wrapped it around his rear axle, then around a tree next to our driveway. When he got up the next morning and went outside to leave for work, he saw the chain, and came running back inside asking me, in a very excited voice, 'Pa, why did you chain up my car?' And, I said, 'Break curfew, be grounded. You can walk to work.'"

"So, Vern did walk to work. Then after work, he went and bought another car. You could get one for only fifty bucks at that time. Sure enough, he drove it home and parked it right beside his chained-up car, proud as punch, thinking he had outsmarted his old man. So, after he went to bed, I went outside and removed the chain from around the tree, to around the axle of both cars. After that, Vern apologized for ignoring curfew and honored it from then on."

"Pretty funny story Grandpa. I recall you also taught my Dad about standing up to a bully too. How did that happen?" I asked.

Again, Grandpa smiled and waited a few moments to reply. He leaned over and took a moment to spit in his tobacco can. "Well, there was this kid at Vern's school that had a reputation for picking on other boys, especially those smaller than him. One day he turned his attention to your Dad and told him after school he was going to beat him up. So, your Dad, not having any experience fighting others, and not anxious to gain any either, slipped out a side door at school and walked towards our house. Unfortunately, this bully, James was his name, saw Vern and took off after him. Well, I was working in the back yard and saw Vern running home, with this other fella chasing him. I could see what was going on by the look on Vern's face. He was scared."

"But I knew he could not do well in life if he let others get the best of him, and now was the time to learn to stand up for himself. So, I waited for Vern on the inside of the gate, with the gate latched on the inside. As Vern arrived, breathless, he jerked on the gate to get on the safe side within his own yard. I stood there and held the gate shut."

"Dad! Let me in! James is going to give me a whipping!" Vern pleaded to me.

"Vern, who would you rather give you a whipping— James, or me?"

"Vern was always a smart boy, and he got the message instantly. Plus, the pride of his Dad, and his own self-respect, was on the line. Vern turned, just as James arrived too, and doubled up his fists and went right at him. James instantly backed off . . . not really wanting to fight someone who showed a willingness to fight back. So, Vern learned his lesson, and never again let a bully scare him."

Grandpa and I continued to talk until late afternoon. Then, I made my excuse and went home, with my mind rolling over the many wonderful stories my Grandpa shared with me. I felt so good for the time we shared, and promised myself we would do this again, and often.

The next morning, I got a phone call early in the morning, just as I was drinking my coffee and reading the morning paper. It was my Dad. He had just gotten a call from Grandma, about Grandpa. She said he went down the driveway to get his morning paper. She heard a loud sound like a gunshot. It made her heart jump! He returned to the house, sat down in his rocking chair, and slumped over. She asked him if someone was shooting at him?

Dan continued, "As he slumped in his rocking chair, he mumbled, 'A car backfired, or someone threw a cherry bomb . . . whatever—damn KKK hellions . . .' He dropped his newspaper and became very still. Gramma sobbed as she told me what happened.

"She felt his pulse, it was quiet, and he was unresponsive. She called me in a panic, very upset, and needs help. I just called for an ambulance."

"Dad, I am coming to your house to pick you up and we will go together. You will need help with this today. I am on my way over to your house now to pick you up."

Dad needed my help for him to deal with this sudden turn of events. As Dad and I drove back over to Grandpa's house, I thought of the irony that I was going there for the second time in two days; after so many years with no visits at all. I thought about my unusual dream that compelled me to go visit him. I felt grateful that I followed my impulse to take time to stay and hear all his wonderful stories. I loved my Grandpa. He was old school, and old-timey in his ideas and ideals. A good way to be.

As Dad and I drove along, we were quiet, each lost in our thoughts, until I turned off Mission Road onto County Line Road. Then, as Dad pointed at a brick cottage on the corner, he said, "Son, that's where I was born."

"Really? I never knew that Dad. I always assumed you were born in the home you grew up in on Wells Drive."

"Well, son, Pa married Ma on February 7, 1917, which was my grandpa's birthday too. I was born on December 3rd[th] of that year. Shortly after that, Pa bought a big lot on Wells Drive, where he and my grandpa Curtis built the house where I grew up. My grandpa, Curtis Bayard Needham, was a home builder, so he knew what he was doing."

I was learning more than I ever knew about my father's early family history, so I asked for more details. "Dad, how did grandpa and gramma meet?"

"My Ma was an orphan at the Shawnee Indian Mission, until she was adopted by Chris and Millie Mikkelsen. They lived in the old north building at the Mission; and my Grandpa Chris ran a dairy operation on land the Mission owned. My Pa, your grandpa, bought milk from Chris and delivered it to a creamery, plus homes and grocers along Rainbow Boulevard to Westport Road. So, one day he asked Katherine, or Ma as we called her, if she would like a ride on his milk wagon? She said, 'Sure'—and the rest is history, as Pa used to say to me. Before he knew it, he had four sons; me, Charles Vernon Needham Junior, Huey, Clarence, and Warren. Or, squirt, squirm, squat, and squeal . . . as Pa nicknamed each of us."

Dad was lost in his memories for a few moments. Yet, I wanted to hear more about my family's early history.

"So, Dad, how old was gramma and grandpa when they got married?"

"My Pa would have been 26 and Ma was 23 years old . . . yep, old enough to know what they were doing," Dad said, with a slight smile. "And, old enough to know better too, as my Pa used to say!"

As we drove into Grandpa's driveway, my eyes were drawn to the two horseshoe pins in front of the deep pits, dug down by many years of pitching horseshoes with Grandpa, and whoever was visiting and willing to pitch horseshoes. I smiled to myself, and remarked to Dad, as I remembered that we could throw the horseshoes a dozen times . . . and finally toss a ringer—then, Grandpa would always toss a ringer right on top of that one. You soon realized he could make a ringer anytime he wanted. But, never one to show off; plus, he knew the value in keeping a game interesting for all the players; he always kept it fun, and interesting for us all.

Dad agreed, his Dad had a big heart. Then I shared with Dad the story Grandpa told me about giving the black fella a ride in his Corliss truck on that snowy winter day. I could see tears well up in my Dads eyes. He was quiet for a moment, then said, "You know son, I wrecked that old Corliss truck once. I was a small boy, and my Dad, Pa, let me go with him to tend to, feed, and milk our small herd of dairy cows.

"I never told you this, but on my first birthday, my grandpa and grandma, Chris and Minnie Mikkelsen; my Ma's adopted parents, gave me a milk-cow. And, Dad bred that cow each year to increase the size of our herd. So, by the time I was ten-years old in 1927, we had ten dairy cows. That kept us in milk, plus extra milk to sell too. Ma always said that really helped us get through the depression. Grandpa and Grandma Mikkelsen were very good people, kind, generous, and with big hearts.

"So, the herd was a couple miles from our home, in a pasture we rented from Mr. Roe, a big landowner in the county. Dad told me to wait in the truck while he finished his chores. Being a curious boy, like most anyone my age, I started pretending I was driving the old truck. I was jerking the levers and suddenly the truck started rolling forward! I had accidently taken it out of park/gear! Well, the old pasture had several deep gulley-ruts running across my path, and soon, the truck rolled right into, and crashed in a deep gulley.

"I was not hurt, just shook up. But I was scared that I was in big trouble and sure to get a licking from your Grandpa. So, I climbed out of the wreck, and saw my Dad walking straight for me, with a stern look on his face. I stood there waiting for the inevitable punishment. But Dad came right up to me, put a hand on each of my shoulders, and looked me square in the eyes, saying, 'Are you okay son?'

"I cried out, 'Dad I am so sorry I wrecked the truck! I was just messing with things . . .!'

"My Dad, still looking in my eyes, and rubbing my joints to make sure nothing was broken, finally said, 'That's okay son. The truck can be repaired or replaced. But, you son, cannot be replaced.'"

Dad and I sat in the car for a few quiet moments, each of us with our own thoughts and memories of my Grandpa. Then, to lighten the mood, I said, "Dad, I can recall, when I was very young, and noticed that Grandpa's house did not have a bathroom—toilet, sink, or bathtub; like we had at home. Just that old outhouse out back, behind the garage. So, I asked Grandpa, "Where does Grandma, you, and your four sons take a bath?"

Well, Grandpa said to me, "Sonny, see the big wash tub handing on the back porch? Well, we put that on the kitchen floor, fill it full of warm water, and sit in it, to take our baths. Yep, we all take a bath, once a year, whether we need one, or not!"

It took me a few years to realize he was joking Dad. But, for a long time I wondered why you did not bath more often? Dad and I laughed at that story as we got out of the car and walked up the drive into the house. We spent the rest of the day making arrangements to say our final farewell to my Grandpa, Charles Vernon Needham.

The next morning, I walked out to my own driveway to retrieve my morning newspaper. Dad and I had made all the funeral arrangements, and family was coming to town from all over the country. I bent down to pick up my newspaper, and as I stood there, I turned to the back pages to scan the obituaries. There it was, Charles Vernon Needham, passed away November 29, 1972.

In that instant, I recalled my dream just a few days earlier. The rush to get to the newspaper's office with Grandpa so he could read the next day's obituary. Tears filled my eyes, as I realized something special had happen, and I have been blessed with a forewarning of something to happen, while there was still time to make a difference. So, this story ends where it began, with a dream, and the chance to make a difference, while there was still time.

The old faucet . . .
(fossil) . . .
My Grandpa Needham.

*My Grandpa & Grandma
Needham, with my dad, Charles V.
Needham, Jr. & Uncle Huey; & the
Corliss truck.*

Hello Mom

What do you do?
When one you've loved the most,
And given all you had to give,
And kept every promise you could,
Turns their back on you.

You search your soul for answers
And find none to help you out.
So, you search your heart for hope,
And find only sadness and despair,
Yet, your soul still yearns for love . . .

So perhaps you write a poem,
To put your feelings into words,
For all the world to know . . .
But the words will not rhyme,
And you're running out of time!

So, you turn your mind from today
To remember a time, when one person
Really knew you, understood you,
And loved you anyway, as they'd wrap
Their arms around you—and you'd say,
"Hello Mom."

—*T. L. Needham*

A RED TAIL GATE

I WAS A homebuilder and developer back in the day. The 1970s to be exact. I had an old '59 Ford pickup truck. It was used for clean-up and trash hauling. It was RED.

A young fella worked for me who wanted to learn the building business. He started at the ground floor—sweeping out the floor of the houses and hauling the trash to the dump, in my RED truck.

The kid's name was Ron, and, well, he had a lot to learn. So, to make his job of emptying the trash out of the truck easier, he removed the tailgate.

I noticed this and saw the tailgate lying loose in the bed of the truck. I realized in an instant that the tailgate might easily slide right off the bed and land in the street. Perhaps even cause a car wreck for someone trying to avoid it. Clearly, Ron could not see into the future, or at least anticipate the future.

So, I said, "Ron, put that tailgate back on the truck before it slides out the back."

Well, the next day I saw Ron with the red truck, and it still had no tailgate attached. Nor was the tailgate in the bed either. It was missing all together! I was more than pissed. I asked Ron where the hell was the tailgate? He said he did not know; it was now missing . . . maybe someone took it?

Later that same day, I stopped by Mom's to visit her. Mom was fighting cancer and near the end of her life. Being the loving mother, she always was, she sensed I was upset about something. So, she asked me what it was, and I told her about my missing tailgate.

Weeks later, Mom was in the hospital . . . in her final hours. I never left her room. The last thing she asked me, before she took her final breath, and went to her eternal home in heaven, was, "Have you found your tailgate son?"

I found it ironic that as my mother was taking her final breaths, the thought in her mind was concern for me, and my problems. That was my mother, always so loving, caring and worrying about me, as well as others.

A few weeks after Mom's funeral, on a Tuesday morning, was my regular sales meeting with my agents. One agent that I had hired recently, Rick was his name, asked to talk with me after the meeting.

As we sat in my office, Rick explained that since I hired him to focus on sales in my subdivision, he wanted a sales office in the subdivision. He liked a small barn, or cabin. He preferred this over holding open our spec houses. And, since we had no model homes at this time, we needed a semi-permanent sales office.

I felt annoyed with this and did not want to incur the expense. Plus, I did not agree with Rick on anything, including not holding open the spec houses in my subdivision. After all, selling the specs is what it was all about.

So, as I shut down the idea, Rick pleaded, if he could please drive me north on the highway to a dealer who sold small barns and portable cabin-houses. He was certain he could persuade me. I was really feeling annoyed at his persistence.

Then, as I was forming the words in my mouth to say, "Not no, but HELL NO!" . . . a quiet voice in my mind, out of nowhere . . . firm, assertive, and strong . . . yet, also gentle, said . . . *"GO WITH RICK!"*

"Oh, all right Rick, if you insist," I said, as we got up and left my office. I got in Rick's car, and we headed north about ten miles up the highway. As we approached the barn/shed/cabin dealer's lot, and we made small talk; a sudden impulse made me turn my head to the right, as far as it would turn. There, in my extreme peripheral vision, way off the road, in dense shade, on a gravel parking lot, by a power station, among a group of cars and trucks, I saw an old 59 Ford Truck painted in grey primer . . . with a BRIGHT RED TAILGATE.

I was shocked and realized some impulse, or a voice, made me say yes to Rick. Now that same impulse made me turn my head clear around to my far right, to see that red tailgate, on a '59 Ford truck, among a crowded lot full of trucks and cars.

So, as soon as Rick and I finished, and I returned to my office, I drove home and got my own '59 red Ford pickup with no tailgate. I drove it ten miles north of town to that parking lot and parked my truck right beside the grey primed '59 Ford truck with the bright red tailgate. I noticed the red tailgate paint matched my own red truck's paint perfectly. Then, I noticed a dealer sticker on the base of the tailgate that matched a dealer sticker on the bumper of my own truck. The dealer was in a very small town in Kansas. So, what are the odds?

Just then, the owner of the grey primed '59 Ford truck with the red tailgate walked up and asked me if he could help me?

In a firm, but friendly manner, I said, "Yes, I believe you have my tailgate on your truck."

The young man noticed the perfectly matching paint on his red tailgate to my red truck. Then, the matching dealer stickers on his tailgate, and my truck.

He said, "You know, I found this tailgate lying in the middle of the road. I thought it was a miracle that I would come across a tailgate for my old '59 truck, which was missing a tailgate. But I can clearly see that this is your tailgate."

We spent the next few minutes removing the tailgate from his truck and putting it back on my own truck. A perfect fit. I thanked the young fella for his honesty and wished him well, as we shook hands and parted.

As I drove home, I felt haunted by my mother's last words to me, asking if I had found my tailgate? Then, I thought of the strong, yet, gentle voice I heard in my mind—urging me to go with Rick; even though I did not agree with his idea and did not want to look at sheds and barns. And, then, the impulse to turn my head clear around to the right to spot that bright red tailgate on a '59 Ford truck; parked so far off the road, in a shady parking lot full of trucks and cars.

I felt certain my mother's hand was guiding these events from heaven; and that I was so blessed that I was compelled to listen, and believe, and follow her message to help me. So, in this story, I learned an important lesson, to listen to your inner voice, and to always be open, and willing, to take the time, like it or not, to follow the guidance whenever, and wherever it leads you. You may never know what wonders await you, until you learn to listen to your guiding voice, and discover who is trying to help you, and with their help—where you are going.

Continuing my drive home, I could not stop thinking about my mother. And, why would I want to? I felt her presence so strong, it seemed she sat beside me in my truck. Mom was the original fount of unconditional love in my life. My mind welled up with images from deep in my memories of our early home. The tiny cottage in Rosedale, Kansas, that backed up to Turkey Creek. The flower garden Mom planted that covered our entire front yard; her favorite, the morning glories that covered the trellis on the side of our porch. The old porch swing where we spent rainy afternoons . . . wishing we could go outside to play.

As I drove along in my truck, one of Mom's favorite classic country songs played on the radio. Mom loved country music, and kept it playing on the radio all day long. Hank Williams, and Patsy Kline, plus others, were her favorite singers. When one of Mom's favorite songs played on the radio, she would start dancing to the tune, no matter what else she was doing at the time. Even as a preschooler, I knew her favorites too. So, when I heard one, I knew Mom was dancing, and we called that— "Mom's doing her routine . . ." Always fun to watch! And, I would peek around the corner, into the kitchen, at Mom dancing in her apron. She would spot me too and pull me into the middle of the kitchen to dance with her . . . as we both did, "Mom's routine." This was such a precious of memories, it made me smile.

I continued to smile to myself as I recalled how hard Mom worked to make our house a home. She even painted the entire outside herself one summer. Mom and dad could not afford to pay a painter, so the only way to get it done was—do it yourself. The same was true inside the house, with Mom's constant stripping of wallpaper and painting of the walls. Dad was gone much of the time since he worked so much overtime on the wrecker crew at the railroad.

Mom would always insist I take a nap in the afternoon, being a four-year old, one needed extra rest. So, she would lay down with me to help me settle off to sleep. I would lie very still, and pretend to be asleep, until I heard my Mom's regular breathing . . . knowing she was the one who worked so hard and really needed a nap. Then I would quietly get up and go outside to play in my sandbox, while Mom got her much needed nap.

It was during my fourth year that I got so upset on Valentine's Day. Mom gave me a wonderful little single-sided Valentine of a panda bear holding a little chalkboard, with a love note written on it. I loved this Valentine so much . . . I started to cry. Mom became distressed at my tears and asked why I was crying? I could not explain as a four-year old that not only did I love my little Valentine card, but also it was my favorite! This is because it was actually the same card Mom had given me the year before, and I remembered it too. So, while Mom thought I was crying because I did not like my Valentine, I could not explain that I was crying because I had just realized that we were so very poor, and Mom did her best to save money, that she had actually re-used last year's Valentines to save that little bit of change.

Being a typical four-year old, I could not wait to be five and start Kindergarten. That day finally came in the late Summer of 1949. Mom walked me up Southwest Boulevard to Holy Name Catholic school. I was beyond words . . . it was so exciting. Once inside the school, we went up a great flight of steps brightly lit by a stained-glass window that rose to the second story level of classrooms. The Sister who taught the Kindergarten class was a beautiful young Nun, named Sister Mildred. I was totally taken by her quiet, reassuring, and sensitive charms. The first lesson she showed our little group of five-year-olds was that she had two small plastic boot-coin banks. One boot was pink for the girls, and the other boot was blue, for the boys. Each day, at the start of class, any kindergartener that had a coin could come forward and put it in the boot-bank of their gender.

I had a minor problem at that age. I had a little speech impediment. I could not pronounce "Bs," or "Ss," or "Ts." In fact, my older sister's name was Sue, and I called her "Tue" . . . which resulted in merciless teasing for me.

Well, I had a new friend in Kindergarten, named Jimmy. I told him I had a penny my Mom gave me because she already knew about the pink and blue boot-banks. I told Jimmy I would be the first boy to put a penny in the "BLUE-POOP-BANK" . . . Jimmy was shocked and protested that he would tell the Sister that I said— "POOP!"

Mortified . . . I pleaded in protest . . . "I did not say 'POOP' . . . I said, 'BPOOPT!'"

This explanation between kindergarteners was no help. My only other option was to start bawling in protest, which I did. As always,

I could not explain to Sister Mildred why I was crying and suddenly Jimmy was tongue-tied too.

Kindergarten lasted a half a day, and we were released at noon. I had been strictly instructed by Mom to come straight home without delay. It was only a three-block walk along the boulevard. Yet, this was actually my first time, on my own, to be loose in the big-wide world. It was fascinating! Across the street from the school and church was a variety store. I stopped in there and looked around for a while. The clerk kept an eye on me and finally asked if I needed help? Feeling his eyes on me . . . I said no and resumed my stroll toward home.

Soon, I came to the blacksmith shop. It was right beside the fire station. This place was amazing! Big horses were standing by, waiting for the attention of the blacksmith. He worked hard over his anvil hammering a chunk of iron into a horseshoe as sparks flew. Finally, he glanced up at me and with a jerk of his head to one side, told me to move on . . .

And, I did, right next door to the fire station, which was a fascinating place with a huge red fire-engine truck. Plus, there were firemen in uniform, sitting out front in their wooden armchairs. One even asked me if I was thirsty? Feeling shy, that I was even noticed, I just nodded— "Yes."

"Well, follow me youngster," as the fireman got up and waved to me to follow him toward the back of the station. There, on the wall, was an Oasis water cooler. It was the first one I had ever seen. I loved ice-cold water. But, clearly, without a step stool, I could not reach the spigot or press the knob to turn on the chilled water flow. So, the kindly fireman gave me a boost to his knee, and I drank my fill. An unforgettable moment of pure pleasure for a five-year old.

Continuing along the boulevard as it took a bend to the right was the bridge over Turkey Creek, and a small cottage. In the front yard there actually was a koi pond. Yes, big golden fish swimming in this small pond. I had no idea how long I stood there starring at the golden koi fish.

Finally, as I walked across the bridge over Turkey Creek, I stopped in the middle of the bridge to lean over the rail and spit in the creek. I had seen my older brother do that many times.

Then, past the bridge, and over the Frisco railroad tracks, was the service station; another place of magical attractions. At the corner of the service station building was a huge stock tank full of water. It was used to check tubes for leaks by pushing them down into the water. This tank was so big that it would hold a tractor tire. But the best part was that it was also full of silver minnows. They were sold for fish bait for those who went fishing in Turkey Creek.

Then a visit inside the service station lead to the popcorn machine. I liked to stick my skinny arm up the popcorn chute to try and tickle out some precious kernels. It would leave my hand covered with salt which I enjoyed licking off.

A few minutes later, I finally arrived at my house, and entered the front door.

"Mom, I'm home!"

Mom emerged from the kitchen—I could instantly see she was in a state of distress. She had tears streaming down her face, and her face was flushed with angst.

'Where have you been? I told you to come straight home after school. What on earth have you been doing? What took you so long to get home! I have been worried sick!" Mom cried and dropped to her knees in front of me. Then she gave me a quick slap across my face! It was the first time she ever struck me.

My nose instantly started bleeding . . . and Mom, feeling responsible for the nosebleed, felt a hundred times worse . . . saying she was so sorry, over and over, as she pulled me close in a hug so tight . . . it was hard to breath.

I wanted so much to explain to Mom that my nosebleed was not her fault! I had been picking my nose all the way home and it was already a little bloody. But I could only join my dear Mother in bawling our hearts out. Consumed with guilt for the entire incident, I resolved to be a good boy and never upset my dear mother again; which was a vow I was destined not to keep.

But I also was becoming fully aware how important it was to be able to express yourself and tell your true feelings. So, as time went by, and I came of age, I was determined to be good at communicating and expressing one's true feelings.

Finally, I reached home in my red truck with the red tailgate now firmly attached. It was time to rejoin the present and let the memories of the past recede back into the memory bank . . . where I keep all of my treasured memories of my Mom.

So, thanks Mom, for the help in finding my lost red tailgate; the precious times we shared, the lessons you taught me, and our mutual, unconditional love . . . *forever.*

My Mother, Geraldine (Jerry)
Theresa Pfeifer-Needham.

That's It!

It is such a small word.
So, I wrote it upon the page,
And just stared at it awhile,
Until it occurred to me
That it could make me smile!
For even it—such a tiny word,
Yet it stands for everything!
And no word works so hard,
But just what does it mean?
It means a lot, or just a little.
And when we are done with it,
Perhaps we shall set it free,
And watch it fly into the sky—
Just to see what it can be . . .
Or, maybe a time will come
When we have all had it . . .
And then just stop it, and say—
That's IT!

—T. L. Needham

THE LITTLE FLOWER GIRL

ANGELA WAS OUTSIDE playing when she heard her mother call to her excitedly, "Angela, come see what I have!" As she ran into the kitchen her mother held up an envelope and said, "Here is a letter from your Cousin Theresa. She is getting married and wants you to be the flower girl in her wedding!"

Angela had no idea what a flower girl was. Actually, she did not know what a wedding was either . . . or what getting married really meant. She was not sure who Cousin Theresa was either, but because her mother was so excited it sounded very exciting to Angela too. In fact, Angela's mother seemed so pleased that she was convinced that this must be a great honor for any little three-year-old girl like herself.

"Well, we will have to buy you a very special dress for the wedding," her mother said. Angela jumped up and down and clapped her hands, as her interest mirrored her mother's.

Several days later, Angela and her mother went shopping for a flower girl dress. They bought a beautiful, full-length, blue satin dress. It had short sleeves that fluffed up so big at the shoulders it made Angela feel like she had wings. Angela twirled and spun around, feeling so happy to see herself in the dressing room mirror wearing this wonderful blue dress.

I look like a princess in a storybook—she thought. Then wondered, *being a flower girl in a wedding must be so special.*

Several weeks passed and soon it was time to drive to the wedding. It took all day to drive from Angela's home in Chicago to Kansas City, where her Grandma and Grandpa lived. Angela and her parents spent the night with them. The next day, they drove to a town called Topeka, in Kansas, for the wedding rehearsal.

Throughout the long trip, Angela wondered what was going to happen. She had not been allowed to wear the beautiful blue dress since her mother bought it. Angela thought about the dress constantly and how special wearing it made her feel. Her mind was full of questions.

"Mommy, what's a rehearsal?"

"It is just like the real wedding, only we practice so that everyone knows exactly what to do and when to do it, so everything will go perfectly at the actual wedding," her mommy replied.

"Like playing make-believe?"

"Yes, dear."

"Will I get to wear my fluffy blue dress at rehearsal?"

"No honey, that dress must not be worn until the actual wedding so it will stay nice and clean."

"Mother, why is the wedding in Topeka?"

"Because that is where your Cousin Theresa lives."

"Mother . . . who is Cousin Theresa? Why do people get married? How soon will we get there . . . how much longer . . . how many minutes . . . are we there yet?"

The questions from Angela came faster than her mother could answer them. Angela's mind was spinning with wonder, and questions about this wedding, and why everyone seemed so excited about it.

Finally, they arrived at the church in Topeka. Angela, happy the long ride was over, anxiously looked out the window to see. As the car pulled up in front of the church, a pretty young woman rushed over to greet everyone in the car.

"Theresa!" Angela's mother exclaimed, "We finally made it . . . You look great! Aren't you excited?" Angela watched her mother and dad climb out of the car as they hugged and greeted Theresa. Angela sat in the back seat of the car, wearing her seat belt, and could barely see out the window.

The car door opened as Theresa leaned over to greet Angela, saying with a rosy-cheeked smile, "So this is Angela! My goodness! What a big girl, and so pretty too." Angela's dad reached across her to unbuckle her seatbelt and then lifted her off the seat and swung around to put Angela on her feet there in front of everyone. Theresa knelt down to Angela's eye-level, saying, "You will be a perfect little flower girl Angela. I am so happy to see you!" Angela saw tears of joy rise in Theresa's eyes and it made her feel happy and kind of sad too, not understanding why the tears? Theresa gave Angela a big hug as she rose to her feet, holding onto Angela.

Feeling a rush of shyness, and not really knowing who Theresa was, Angela squirmed and reached for her mommy or daddy, with a little whine. Feeling like a small doll being hugged by a big girl, Angela felt overwhelmed. Theresa sensed this and put Angela down on her feet, as they all chatted and Theresa led them into the church, Angela's dad picked her up and carried her, as he whispered, "Theresa is your cousin who is getting married. The wedding will be wonderful and fun, I promise."

In the church, there were more people to meet too. Angela was introduced to Johnny, who was to be the bridegroom. She was told that meant he was the person her Cousin Theresa was going to marry. Then Angela was introduced to Theresa's father, her Uncle Chuck. He said it was nice to see her again, but she was only three years old and not sure she remembered meeting him before. He did seem to be very nice. He went on to explain that he was her daddy's brother, so that made him her uncle. He also said he was the one who would, "give the bride away." That sounded very strange and confusing to Angela. She wondered, *why was her uncle Chuck going to give his daughter, Theresa, away—didn't he like her anymore?*

Everyone walked into the church. There was more hugging, hand shaking, and people making introductions. Theresa brought over a tall thin man, dressed in black slacks and a black shirt with a thin white collar, to meet Angela.

"Angela, this is our minister, Reverend Mark. He is going to perform the wedding ceremony tomorrow. Now he is going to tell each of us just what we are to do during the ceremony, then we will practice that several times. Doesn't that sound like fun?"

Reverend Mark smiled at Angela through his thick glasses that made his eyes look too big for his face. He gently touched her on the cheek and said warmly, "Angela, it is very nice to meet you. You look like a very bright child. I am certain you will do just fine." He had a deep voice and reassuring manner that made Angela feel more comfortable. He then extended his hand to shake Angela's hand. She reached up and took hold of one finger as he gave her hand a gentle squeeze.

Angela wondered if Reverend Mark was a magician since he was dressed in black and was going to "perform the ceremony" that would make the marriage happen. She liked magicians and magic. She knew about magicians because her older brother Mark was always showing her magic tricks. Angela was pretty certain Reverend Mark was also a magician, so, this wedding was getting more interesting.

Reverend Mark took charge of everything. He told everyone exactly what was going to happen and when it would happen. Then he took people aside individually and told them again exactly what they were to do, when they were to do it, and where they should be when they did it.

Soon it was Angela's turn for instructions from Reverend Mark. He spoke with gentle kindness as he explained that this was a very special and wonderful event for Theresa and Johnny. It was also a very special event for all of their families and friends too. Reverend Mark said this was a celebration of love between two people and a very happy time for them, as well as for everyone else. He assured Angela that there was nothing to be afraid of, to listen closely, and he would tell her exactly what to do.

Angela was mesmerized by his deep, soft voice and his kind, reassuring manner. She was certain he must be a magician. He took her by the hand with one of his fingers and walked her over to the big double doors at the entrance to the church. There they stood. Looking down a long aisle leading to the front of the church and the altar. Reverend Mark knelt down on one knee and leaned close to Angela. She was listening very carefully.

"Angela, you have the most important job in this wedding. Do you know why?"

Angela slowly turned her head side to side to indicate, *no, she did not know why.*

"You have the most important job in this wedding, Angela, because as the flower girl, you will lead the bride into the church. And, you will prepare her path by dropping rose petals each step along the way. You are the first person in the wedding party to enter the church. Don't you agree this is a very important job, Angela?"

Angela slowly moved her head up and down to indicate, yes.

Even as Angela tried to listen closely, she had no idea what he was talking about. She did realize, though, that since everyone was so excited about this wedding that it must be a big deal, and she understood that she would have to try hard to do what was expected of her. But most of all, Angela wanted to make everyone proud of her, especially her parents.

Reverend Mark then told Angela she should pretend she was holding a little basket full of rose petals. He held his hand out in front of him as if he was holding a basket of rose petals.

"Angela, you will take one step, pause, bring both feet together like this . . . drop a rose petal . . . take a step . . . pause, both feet together . . . drop a petal, and so on until you get all the way down the aisle to the altar."

Reverend Mark walked a few steps down the aisle, showing her exactly what to do. He looked so funny to Angela that she wanted to laugh, but she didn't because everyone was watching and seemed so very serious.

She proceeded down the aisle several steps behind Reverend Mark. Each one of them stepping forward, then a pause, bringing both feet together . . . drop a petal from the make-believe basket . . . then step forward on the other foot. Over and over they did this until they reached the end of the aisle and stood in front of the altar.

Angela had a hard time not getting the giggles as she followed this tall, skinny man dressed in black with his thick glasses doing this silly walk down the aisle of the church.

Reverend Mark then knelt down and placed a dime on the carpet just three steps to the left of the aisle. He whispered to Angela, "You did that perfectly dear. Next, you step to the side of the aisle and stand right on top of this dime. You must keep this dime covered throughout the entire wedding, no matter how long it takes, and you must stand very still and quiet too. Can you do that my dear?"

Angela nodded her head up and down.

"Perfect! I knew you were a bright child!"

Then Reverend Mark asked Angela to practice standing still and covering the dime while they finished the rehearsal. Angela did just that. It was very boring. She spent the time wondering what the real wedding would be like, what it was all about, and how much fun it was going to be wearing that beautiful blue dress again.

After the rehearsal, there was a party at the house where Johnny's parents lived. There was a lot of good food, candy, cake and soda pop. Most importantly, there were other children there for Angela to play with. There were also many grown-up people that Angela did not know, and her daddy kept introducing her to, over and over again.

Now she was having fun. Her father was playing a game called "pool" with some other guests. It looked like fun. They were poking brightly colored balls with long sticks called cues. They kept tapping the balls and making them ram into one another and roll all over the table. Occasionally, a ball would roll into one of the pockets at each corner or on the side of the table, then drop out of sight, as everyone cheered and got very excited.

It looked like so much fun Angela asked her father if she could do it too. Her father said, "Sure!" He bent down in front of Angela, held the cue stick in front of a big white ball and said, "Now Angela, push the cue against the ball."

She gave the cue a big push: *bang—click—bump—kerplunk.* One of the balls disappeared into a corner pocket.

"Great shot!" her father exclaimed as others yelled their approval too.

"Can I do it again, Daddy? Please?" Angela asked, looking up and grinning at her daddy.

"No honey, not again. It is late and time for us to go home. We have a long drive tonight and again tomorrow to return for the wedding. You must get to bed so you will be well rested for your big day tomorrow, right?"

As Angela and her parents were leaving the party, a heavy rain began to fall. They ran splashing across the street as her father carried her to the car. They drove the turnpike back to Kansas City; as Angela fell asleep to the rhythmic beat of the windshield wipers, and the gentle patter of rain drops on the car roof.

Angela slept late the next day. Everyone did. They were very tired after the long drive from Chicago, then on to Topeka, and then rehearsal, and the party afterwards. Now it was time to wake up and get ready for the real wedding, later today.

Everyone was very excited as they showered, washed their hair, and put on their very best clothes. Angela's mother took special pains to help Angela. She carefully brushed her hair until it was just so, then placed a big blue-ribbon right-on top of her head.

Later, when Angela and her parents arrived at the church, dark storm clouds were gathering. The radio announcer had just warned there was a severe weather alert for the Topeka area with a chance of a tornado. Angela was not sure what a tornado was, but she knew from the way her parents became very quiet, and listened closely to the radio, that it was a very scary thing to have happen.

As Angela and her parents entered the church, one of the bridesmaids offered to show them to the dressing rooms for the wedding party. Once in the dressing room, Angela was at last allowed to put on the beautiful blue gown that was her little flower girl dress. Angela looked at herself in the mirror and easily imagined that she was a princess, or even an angel with wings as she stared, then twirled around with joy at the big fluffy sleeves. The dress gave her a very special, almost magical, feeling.

Angela Marie Noelle Needham—
The Little Flower Girl.

Her mother fussed with Angela's hair a little more. Everyone was getting nervous, and with each minute Angela could feel the excitement in the room growing. Soon it was time for the wedding to begin. Angela was taken to the entrance at the back of the church by her mother who was then escorted to her place in a pew at the first row of the church. She would be sitting right behind the spot where Angela was going to stand on the dime during the wedding ceremony.

Angela was told to wait at the back of the church and stay by her Uncle Chuck, the bride's father. Angela remembered that he was the one who was going to "give the bride away"—although she still did not understand what that meant. Uncle Chuck would tell her what to do, and when to do it. Plus, her mother and father were going to be waiting for her at the end of the aisle.

Just then, the lights in the church went out, but only for an instant. There was a very low, heavy rumble of thunder in the distance. Angela felt a little rush of fear—others nearby gasped from the unexpected moment of darkness. The storm seemed to be getting nearer.

As Angela stood there in the doorway to the church looking down the aisle, she began to realize that nothing was the same as the rehearsal—everything was different, and very frightening. The church was dark, with only candlelight glowing from each pew along the aisle and the candles on the altar at the end of the aisle. The church was full of strangers, all dark silhouettes against the glow of candlelight. Angela's fear began to swell into panic within . . . she wanted her mommy and daddy. She strained to see them down the aisle inside the dark church, but only the stare of strangers met her searching eyes.

Suddenly, loud organ music began to play. The sound filled the church. The thunder from the storm rumbled again and lightening flashed beyond the church windows. A thought raced through Angela's mind that she should run and hide, or find her parents, but she was frozen with fear.

The church organist began to play the Wedding March. Lightning flashed in the windows and thunder vibrated the church again. Uncle Chuck knelt down beside Angela and handed her a small white basket full of rose petals. The sweet scent of the rose petals along with Uncle Chucks' calm voice helped her be a little less frightened.

He smiled as he gave Angela the basket of rose petals and spoke in her ear, so she could hear him above the loud organ music and thunder, "Now it is time for you to lead the wedding procession by dropping these rose petals for the bride's path." Angela understood and knew what she was supposed to do.

Angela turned and looked down the aisle. Lightening flashed in the church windows again, revealing the crowd of strangers who were all staring at her. The organist played even louder as if the sound of the music alone would sweep Angela down the aisle. In that instant, everyone in the church stood up, making a sudden roaring sound, and all eyes fell upon tiny three-year-old Angela. The crowd towered over her, this little flower girl, in her beautiful blue gown, holding a basket of rose petals. Angela knew it was time to begin. But she did not move . . . she could not move—it was just too terrifying!

Uncle Chuck gently urged little Angela, telling her that her mother and father were waiting at the end of the aisle for her. The Bride, Theresa, who also looked nervous and frightened, held her breath.

Everyone in the church looked down on the frightened little flower girl. Hope swelled in each person's heart that this tiny little child could find the courage to come forward and lead the way for the bride. Even the Reverend Mark at the head of the aisle, behind the altar, held out his arms and smiled a gentle smile at Angela as he beckoned her to come to him.

Angela's father was kneeling, halfway down the aisle, with his camera so he could take pictures of her in the beautiful blue flower girl dress. He quietly urged Angela to come forward and motioned to her with his outstretched arms.

Angela's mother waited in the first pew. She understood the delay and knew her little daughter was overwhelmed with fear. Her mother hoped with all her heart that Angela would find the courage to overcome her fear.

But the little flower girl did not move. The dark church . . . the candlelight . . . the strangers . . . the huge crowd . . . the loud organ music . . . the thunder and lightning—it was all just too much! And, where was her mother and father? She could not see them! She really just wanted to run away and cry!

Angela felt a hard lump growing in her throat and it hurt to swallow. Tears welled up in her eyes and one began to run down her cheek.

Then, just as everyone was about to give up on the little flower girl leading the bride down the aisle, Angela brushed the tear aside with her small white-gloved hand, and bravely stepped forward. Thunder rumbled—lightening flashed again—and in the same instant, everyone in the church gave a long sigh of relief with admiration sparkling in their eyes for Angela, the brave little flower girl.

She reached into her white basket and grabbed a fist full of rose petals, just as she pretended to at the rehearsal. Then she paused, brought both feet together, and stepped forward again, dropped one big clump of rose petals, and then quickly walked down the aisle.

Everyone was now focused on the bride, as she began her procession down the aisle. It was her big moment and the crowd quickly forgot about the little flower girl walking up the aisle, alone, and not dropping little clumps of rose petals. They forgot about her great fear, and even greater courage to face those dreadful things that surrounded her. Yet, Angela had done what she was asked to do, and the wedding ceremony was more wonderful for her beauty, courage and charm.

Near the middle of the aisle, Angela met her father, who was kneeling in the aisle taking pictures. She stepped toward him, handed him the little white basket asking with her eyes if should could just stop now and sit down.

Her daddy hugged her, and whispered, "You are so brave, and I am very proud of you. You are doing fine Angela, just continue down the aisle and stand on the dime just like you did at the rehearsal. Mother is waiting for you right there in the front pew."

That helped Angela. At least now she knew where her mother and father were and realized that her ordeal was almost over. She remembered the dime on the floor that the minister had placed there and asked her to stand on top of it until the ceremony was over.

So, Angela hurried down the aisle . . . *not dropping rose petals along the way.* Soon she saw her mother smiling at her from the front pew. She had tears of pride and joy in her eyes as she watched her beautiful and brave little daughter.

Then Angela reached the end of the aisle and looked to her left for the dime she was supposed to stand on. It was not there—*Oh no! What was she to do? How would she know she was standing in the right spot?* She wondered . . . Well, no one seemed to be watching her anyway since all eyes were now focused on the bride, who was following her down the aisle. Angela decided perhaps Reverend Mark simply forgot to put the dime down. Grown-ups do forget things, she knew that. So, the little flower girl pretended a dime was sitting on the floor, just where she remembered it was supposed to be. She stepped on top of the make-believe dime and stood there for the rest of the ceremony.

Now, for the first time, Angela looked back behind her, and up the aisle she had just walked down. She saw the one little pile of rose petals she had dropped. Then she saw her Cousin Theresa, the bride. She was dressed in a long, flowing white satin dress that seemed to glow in the dim candlelight of the church. She was smiling a teary, but happy smile of nervous joy. She held the arm of her father, Angela's Uncle Chuck, who was so gentle and understanding when Angela had her fearful moment of hesitation before she began. It was a beautiful moment as the organ music continued to fill the church, and the hearts of all those present with the wonderful Wedding March music. Angela now began to feel and understand the joy and excitement about the wedding. She also began to understand why being a little flower girl in a wedding was such a special honor. Angela felt the very strong presence of love in the church in the way that only small children can feel so clearly. Angela knew the magic was now happening.

As the beautiful bride passed by Angela, who was looking up

at her with eyes full of wonder, she smiled down at Angela and whispered a quiet, "Thank you." Angela smiled to herself and felt proud that she found the courage to do her part. She stood very still throughout the rest of the wedding ceremony and watched every moment with great interest.

After the wedding, a party was held in the hall beneath the church. Everyone was happy and had a good time. There was a huge white cake with little statues of the bride and groom on top. Plus, refreshingly cold pink punch was served, and rosebud candy mints.

Angela had several servings of the cake and punch, and no one knows for sure how many mints she ate. She was so happy and excited that she took off her shoes and danced all over the reception hall in her stocking feet. She twirled around and around with her arms stretched out. Then she would disappear into the crowd, work her way to the front of the line and sneak another mint . . . or two. She would weave through the crowd to watch her Cousin Theresa and Johnny, her new husband, who sat opening presents and laughing joyfully. After peaking at them for a moment, Angela would feel another rush of joy and excitement and spin back out into the reception hall, dancing and twirling about in her bare stocking feet.

Finally, it was time to go home. Cousin Theresa came over to Angela, who by now was quite tired and sitting quietly beside her father and mother. Theresa thanked Angela for being in her wedding as the beautiful little flower girl. She handed Angela a gift wrapped in shiny white paper with a big white ribbon tied into a big bow. Theresa told Angela she could keep the little flower girl basket too, as a special souvenir of the wedding! Angela was thrilled with the thought of having that little white basket too. It just seemed to belong to her along with her wonderful blue flower girl dress.

Angela wanted to wait until she was in the car to open her present. So, her father walked her to the car while her mother looked for the little flower girl's basket.

Once in the back seat of the car, Angela unwrapped her gift from Theresa. It was a pair of pretty lacy barrettes with long yellow ribbons hanging down. Angela loved them. However, she really wanted her little flower girl basket too. Soon, her mother returned to the car and explained that everyone had tried to find the little white flower basket—it could not be found. It was lost in all the excitement and confusion after the wedding. Perhaps someone had taken it by mistake. Angela was very sad that it was now lost.

As her family drove back home to Chicago, Angela thought how much fun it was to be a little flower girl. Even though it seemed so scary at first. That was all over now. She remembered how proud and pleased everyone seemed to be with her. She also remembered feeling the love and excitement of the wedding and felt she understood more about marriage and how families came together. It was such a magical and wonderful ceremony of love and family unity. She wondered about her own parent's wedding and wished she could have been their little flower girl too.

Angela remembered the white cake, the pink punch, and most of all, those delicious rosebud mints. She remembered the heavenly music and dancing in her stocking feel all over the reception hall. She remembered the nice present Theresa had given her. But, most of all, she remembered the little white basket that was now hers, but lost. Oh, she missed that little white basket and wanted it so much.

She slowly drifted off into a very tired, but happy sleep.

One afternoon several weeks later, back home in Chicago, Angela was playing dress-up in her glorious blue flower girl dress. She danced and twirled all about the house. Her yellow barrettes held her hair back as the long flowing ribbons danced about her face. Then she heard the doorbell ring. It was the mailman with a package for Angela. Inside the package was a note that her mother read to her:

"Dear Angela,

Your flower girl basket was packed with my presents by mistake. So, I am sending it to you. Thank you again for being my beautiful little flower girl.

Love,
Cousin Theresa"

Angela was so thrilled to have her little flower girl basket again, that she screamed and jumped with joy. Holding the little basket in her hands, she twirled and danced all about the house, pretending she was once again the beautiful little flower girl.

AFTER MIDNIGHT

THE GREAT FLOOD of 1951 swamped Kansas City on Friday, July 13th, 1951. That was also the day after I turned 7 years old. It was a major disaster with great loss of life, livestock, and property. I mean the flood, not my birthday, which was just another hot, muggy day that July when it seemed to never stop raining.

My dad, Vern, worked for the railroad and they got hit the hardest since all railroad yards were in the "bottoms" and went underwater. It took many weeks of arduous labor and determination, plus long backbreaking hours, to get the railroad lines open again. The economic life of the city and much of the country depended on the trains moving.

Our own home, in Rosedale, backed up to Turkey Creek and came very close to going under water. Our backyard flooded all the way up to the first step of our porch. So, Mom and Dad had vowed to move the family to higher ground. It was exciting for us children to look at homes with them and try to imagine which room we might get to call our own. That is, if, we got a room of our own. My brother and I now shared a room, and my two sisters slept on the studio sofa that folded out into a bed in the living room.

Yet, there was one truly memorable evening that stands out for me in those days. Late that summer, my Dad's union, The Brotherhood of Railway Carmen, held a party to celebrate and reward their members for their grueling hard work that followed the flood. It was held in a spacious tavern on Southwest Boulevard. The place had a long bar across the back, a room full of pool tables off to one side, and the main room full of tables and chairs, plus my favorite, a jukebox.

All the walls were covered with mirrors, or neon beer signs, or various liquor ads that gave the place a carnival atmosphere. But the sounds were the best part . . . the clinking of bottles and glasses, the steady undertow of chatter, punctuated with the outburst of laugher, or a yell at someone from across the room, or a plea to the bartender to "set up another round" and the music. Yes, the music . . . over all the noise and pandemonium, the booming music ruled from the nickelodeon, or, jukebox, as it was called.

The song being played the most, it turns out, was already my favorite—as Teresa Brewer's cheerful girly voice pleaded:

Put another nickel in . . .
In the nickelodeon . . .
All I want is having you . . .
And "Music! Music! Music!"

I had already heard that song, *"Music! Music! Music!"* played on our car radio, and television at home, since it was a hit sweeping the nation. Plus, the lovely Teresa Brewer had become my idea of the ideal woman, along with my own mother.

The beat was irresistible, and I found myself doing my own seven-year old version of the "hokey-pokey" in front of the wonderful jukebox. My eyes were fixed on the bubbles rising in multi-colored tubes running up the sides and over the top of the nickelodeon.

Then I noticed someone was stepping off a stool right in the middle of the crowded bar. The space left by the empty stool allowed my eyes to fall upon the only thing that could distract me from the wondrous light and music show of the jukebox—a "gumball" machine. Yes, there it sat, right in the center of the bar, loaded with my favorite color of gumballs, bright red!

I dug my fists in my jean-pockets in search of a penny, or two. Alas, nothing but lint filled my fingers as I withdrew them. I searched the crowded tables to seek out my parents. Spotting them, I rushed over and pleaded to mom, who was usually a generous source of pennies, or even a nickel now and then.

"Mom, could I have a penny, or two, PLEASE?"

I could see Mom was in a wonderful and happy mood. She and Dad were sipping drinks and laughing at the funny stories told by Dad's best friend, Tyke Juliano. They worked together, and Tyke played baseball with the local Argentine team and we often watched him play at Shawnee Park in Armourdale in the west bottoms of Kansas City, Kansas. All that area was under water during the recent flood. Tyke and his family lived on Strawberry Hill overlooking the Union Pacific Railroad yards, where he and my dad worked. We always had a great time when our families came together.

Mom opened her purse, then pulled out her coin purse and unzipped it. She counted out five pennies and without asking why, just smiled her beautiful smile at me and winked, "There honey, now you go have fun, but stay out of trouble."

My fist gripped tightly around the five pennies, I saddled up on the bar stool in front of the red penny-gumball machine. I had to sit upon my knees, folded on my legs, to be high enough to reach the slot to slip in a penny. Then I took a tight grip on the lever and pulled it across the machine. Sure enough, a shiny red gumball dropped down into the slot. However, the instant I retrieved my treat, I realized something was not right. This bright red gumball was made of plastic and had a hole in it! Stuffed within the hole was a tightly folded piece of paper. I felt cheated.

"Here sonny, use this to poke that paper out, and let's see what hand you've drawn." As I heard this quaky old voice; and he handed me a matchstick. I turned and looked up to my left. An old-timer with puffy eyes that twinkled under his bushy eyebrows, and gray hair revealed that he had not seen a barber in months. He was wearing a ragged old Union Pacific blue pin-striped hat on his head. Giving this stranger the once over, I could see he was wearing bibbed coveralls, just like my dad always wore to work. He wore a denim blue cotton shirt that had not seen an iron for as long as the barber had missed his hair. I stared at the old timer, then the match, as I no doubt looked dumbstruck, because I was.

"Let me show you how this works young man," the old fella said, again with the soft quaky voice. He raised his other shaky old veined hand to take the red ball out of my hand. Then, with both hands shaking, he used the match end to push the folded paper out of the red ball, which I realized now looked more like a bead than a gum ball. Then, with his big old calloused fingers shaking, he slowly unfolded the tiny strip of paper. "There you are sonny, let's see what your hand is . . ." Holding the paper away from his eyes far enough to find his focus range, he exclaimed, "Well sonny, you are a lucky young fella. You have hit a payoff on your first hand. Let me show you how this works. You see those five symbols? Each one is a card, and then you check your five cards against this little chart, right on top of that gumball machine. Now you can see that you have two-of-a-kind in your hand, which equals 'one-pair' which makes you a winner."

For the first time, I noticed there was a chart on top of the gumball machine. I strained my neck to get close enough to see a list of poker hands and the payoff on each hand:

One Pair = 5 cents
Two Pair = 1 dime
Three of a Kind = 1 quarter
Straight = 50 cents
Flush = 75 cents
Full House = 1 dollar
Four of a Kind = 2 dollars
Straight Flush = 5 dollars
Royal Flush = 10 dollars

"Bartender! We have a winner here, pay this young man!" I was trying to comprehend all this new information about poker hands, as the old timer called out to the bartender. The bartender glanced our way and finished setting up several drinks he was working on, then wiped his hands on the bar towel and walked over to us. "Show him what you've got there sonny," as the old timer pointed at the tiny strip of paper in my hand. I reached it over to the bartender.

He snatched it out of my fingers with an air of irritation and held it up to the light. "Well, kid, this must be your lucky night," as he turned his back to me and opened the cash register behind the bar. Then, turning back toward me, he reached over and dropped five pennies on the bar, and walked away.

I was thrilled to have more money to put in the machine. My five new pennies, plus four left that Mom had given me, now felt like a treasure. I said nothing—but glanced a smile of appreciation to the old timer sitting beside me. He winked and took a long swig on his beer.

So, it went for several hours, with time marked only by the insertion of a penny, then sliding the level across to release the little red plastic poker-hand bead-gumball. Over and over again, as a puddle of empty red beads grew on the bar in front of me. Beside it was a pile of useless paper poker hands to the left, and my small stack of pennies on the right. Every time my stack of change dwindled down to a few remaining pennies, I would hit a wining hand, and stay in the game. Meanwhile, beyond my focused and determined effort to play out this game, the party continued in the background.

Eventually, as I began to grow a little weary, and a lot discouraged, I realized my penny-pile was nearly gone, and so were the red gumballs in the glass domed machine. I leaned forward to see what remained in the machine. Only three little red gum balls remained. I stared at my stack of pennies and saw only three pennies remained. I took a deep sigh, and slipped another penny into the slot, pushed the lever across, took the red plastic gumball and poked out the poker hand with the now well-worn matchstick. Nothing. Another bust, a loser, no payoff. Quickly and with determined resolve, I picked the second to the last penny and repeated the now familiar ritual. Nothing. Another loser. Only one penny remained. Only one red plastic gumball remained in the bottom of the machine.

I paused, and for the first time in several hours, glanced over to the shaggy old man who had been sitting beside me all this time. I saw four empty beer bottles in front of him, and one in his hand as he took another long swig. As he slowly lowered the bottle to the bar, he realized I was staring at him, for the first time since my long poker game against the machine began.

"Well, sonny, looks like your luck has held up to the very end. Or has it?" His quaky voice whispered with a slight slur. "Well, take it from me young fella, winning is more about 'will' than 'luck' . . . believe in yourself and make it happen." Then he raised his brown longneck bottle of beer and drained it, and yelled, "Jake, I'm dry over here!"

That was the first time I heard the bartender called by name. I watched him as he looked our way, and shook his head, as if to say, *what a pain in the neck those two are tonight.*

It took that long for the old man's words to soak in, and with a renewed and determined "will to win" . . . I picked up my last penny and shoved it in the slot. Across the front I slid the lever and took the last little red gum-ball-poker hand in my fingers. I pushed out the paper poker hand with my trusty matchstick. Then I slowly pulled the paper open and studied the contents. There were five cards printed. They were all the same color. I had not seen one like this before. I studied the chart. WOW! This hand was a 'flush' as in all five cards of the same kind . . . and, then I realized, they were all in a series, which meant, yes . . . this was a "straight-flush" which paid five dollars . . . No, as my eyes reached the top of the chart and I saw the words, "Royal-Flush"— and then realized that image on the chart was an exact match to the hand I was holding . . . A ROYAL FLUSH. So, what was the payoff for that hand? I instantly wondered as I strained my neck to read the very top right-hand side of the chart on top of the gum ball machine—TEN DOLLARS!

"HEY JAKE! I got a ROYAL FLUSH!" I yelled at the top of my squeaky seven-year old voice. I waved my little tag of paper with this wonderful poker hand treasure. Jake stopped what he was doing and with a worried and shocked expression on his face, walked over and snatched the poker hand paper from my hand, "Let me see that kid."

Jake studied the hand for a long moment, then he held it up to the light . . . and shook his head as he handed it back to me, saying, "Sorry kid, we only pay these Royal Flush winners on Sunday."

Instant heartbreak sank in, as I realized this was Saturday night and this bar, nor any bar, was even opened on Sunday in this town. Tears began to well up in my eyes with the sudden disappointment; I could feel my lower lip begin to pout out, as I tried to choke back the tears.

"Wait a minute sonny, this isn't over yet, let me see that hand. The grisly old-timer took the paper strip from my fingers. "Yep, this is the real deal, sonny." Then he bellowed, "JAKE! GET YOUR ASS OVER HERE!"

Jake had slipped off toward the end of the bar and was trying to look busy, but when summoned by the old man, he reluctantly walked back to ask, "What?"

"So, you agree this is a Royal-Flush and it is a ten-dollar payoff, but you only payoff these hands on Sunday, right?" The old-timer growled.

"Yep, you heard me right old-timer," Jake replied with a stubborn resolve.

"Well, you jackass, turn around and look what time it is . . . Today is now Sunday because it is ten minutes past midnight," the old-timer growled again.

Jake got a look on his face like he had just been slapped, and deserved it too, as he slowly turned around to see the clock on the wall above the bar did, in fact, read ten minutes past midnight. Then, he slipped his hand in his pocket and double-checked the time on his pocket watch. Next, slowly shaking his head back and forth, he punched a key on the cash register to open the cash drawer and retrieved a crisp ten-dollar bill. He turned, handed it to me, while he glared at the old timer, then his eyes fell on me and he said, "Now beat it kid."

I gripped the crisp ten-dollar bill with both hands, looked up at the old timer, who reached over and briskly rubbed my hair on top of my head. I was too choked up to say the much deserved, "THANK YOU!" But that is what I felt in my heart, as I slid off my stool. I hope the look in my eyes showed the old timer my gratitude. I searched the room for my parents, and seeing them, ran off yelling, "Mom, Dad, I won, I won, I won ten-dollars!"

Yes, these moments of my early childhood were destined to be unforgettable. I would never forget how I learned the lessons that persistence is one key to winning, and so is luck, plus a "will-to-win" is essential, and it is always good to have a little help from a well-meaning friend too. But most important of all, you must always want . . . *time to be on your side too.*

The Eternal Moment

The past exists
Only in a memory . . .
The future exists
Only in a dream . . .
Only the moment is real.
Do not let it pass—unfulfilled.
Memories can fade,
And dreams may perish . . .
But now, this instant, is reality!
This constant moment—*is eternal.*

—*T. L. Needham*

MOONGLOW TAVERN
MEMORIES

THE MOONGLOW TAVERN, is a go-go joint, with a long and narrow room, lined with a bar running the length on the right; an aisle between the bar and stools, with a row of booths and tables along the left wall. The go-go stage is against the wall at the far end of the room. The place is packed late on Friday night.

I am there with a couple of buddies after working the night shift. As we enjoy our drinks, banter, and the go-go dancer; the front door swings open, bringing a blast of frigid air and snowflakes into the place. Standing in the doorway is an older gentleman who looks totally out of place. He looks like a refugee from some old black and white film noir of the 1940s. He is wearing a Fedora, perfectly formed and fit, tilted slightly to right over his ear, covering the white hair that was perfectly trimmed. He has a thin moustache, dark rimmed glasses, clean shaved face, with a starched white-collar shirt, graced with a maroon silk tie, covered by a perfectly fitted wool overcoat, revealing pin-striped wool slacks pressed to a sharp crease down the front. Closing this image, was his pair of polished black Florsheim shoes. In short, he looked totally out of place in this rough and tumble blue-collar joint.

So, as the front door swung open to reveal this misplaced soul, that blast of cold north wind follows him, bringing a chill and snowflakes that stopped the music for a moment, and each hapless soul in the joint looked his way for an instant . . . wondering, are you a cop? Looking for me? A private eye my wife hired to keep an eye on me? The bill collector I have been dodging for months, here to repossess my car? Or worst, a mild-mannered, yet deceptive appearing hit man that bookie you owe has sent to finally settle your bill, once and for all. That instant passed as quickly as it arrived, and everyone turned to their drinks and laughs, as the go-go dancer swiveled her hips in the most hypnotic rhythm.

The stranger did not pause at the door long enough to even survey the room. What he was after was clear as he moved into the noisy crowded bar. He sought space at the bar in this packed asylum of refugees from their daily grind. He found his space right in the middle of my friends and myself.

"Excuse me my man, pardon me. Bartender, a tall bourbon on the rocks, if you please, and set up my friend here too," he ordered, as he winked at me, in appreciation for making room for him at the bar.

Shocked that he ordered a drink for me, evidently in appreciation for stepping back to allow him to squeeze up to the bar, I recovered quickly from my surprise and asked, "Hey, thank you my man, but what about my two buddies here too?" The distinguished Fedora topped gentleman, was already taking a long pull on his bourbon as he turned, still holding the amber iced glass of bourbon, now half empty, and said graciously, "Of course my good man, of course, bartender, set up each of these good men, if you please, and pour one for you too, my good man!"

"Well, thanks old timer. But what keeps you out so late and how did you find this little hell-hole full of Satin's rejects?"

"My good man, I've worked for the railroad, thirty years now, if you can imagine that. I have risen . . . Yes, I have risen, just as our savior has risen, quite miraculously to the top of my firm's ladder. And, I just arrived from a week in New York, where I closed a major merger deal with another railroad into our own." He drained his bourbon and turned to slam his glass on the bar loud enough to catch the eye of the bartender.

"Hey Jack!" I shouted at the bartender. "A quick reload here for my friend, and three more for his posse here too!" Jack, the bartender knew me well, and as our eyes met, he rolled his eyes and shook his head slightly, as I read his lips when they silently mouthed to me the response, "JERK!"

The first bourbon primed my distinguished new friend's voice, and he quickly took a gulp of the second, as he continued to tell his story of triumph in New York.

However, I was distracted from listening as the door to the joint opened once again, bringing the same frosty blast of air and snowflakes.

In the doorway stood a tall, burly man, with the bulk of a prize fighter, wearing a cap with a union badge pinned on the side, a leather bombers jacket, and scruffy looking trousers. Again, all eyes fell upon him in that instant, as each soul pondered the impact this newcomer may have on them. He quickly moved in, shoved his way with a determined flow through the crowd, right up to my new patron and two friends. He thumped the well-dressed old patron on the back of his shoulder with considerable vigor. Startled, the old man turned to look up at this new grizzly looking man, as he said,

"Say fella, I been waiting in my cab out there for twenty minutes now. Your bill for the ride from the train station to here, plus that extra twenty minutes, is now over fifty bucks. So, you coming out or what?"

"Now, now, my dear man. Please, join us. Have a drink with us. We're in no hurry. What's your pleasure?" The old man asked the cab driver, with an edge of a slur in his speech, as the bourbon was already going to work.

"No old man. I am on duty; you know that—for crying out loud! I will be waiting in the cab, but just don't forget. The meter is running,"

He turned, and as a snowplow would, he pushed his way through the crowd, and back out the front door. Only a moment or two passed, but no sooner was he forgotten, then the tavern door swung open again with more force than before, along with same blast of frigid air and snowflakes. There again stood the burly hulk of a man, who was glaring as he fixed his gaze upon the old man, my two buddies, and myself.

"What on earth?" was the only comment I made as I watched this bulk of a man push his way past the crowd and right up to the old gentleman, as he said, "Hey old man, your bill just went up two thousand dollars! Cause while I was in here farting around with you, someone stole my cab!"

"Jack, call the cops, quick! This guy's cab was just stolen!" and then I turned my eyes to the cabbie, with sincere sympathy and concern, asked, "Look fella, that is terrible. The cops will be here in a moment. So, how about that drink after all?"

The cabbie rolled his eyes, shrugged his massive shoulders and said, "What the Hell! Give me a beer."

"Jack! A beer for this good man, and quick please!" I was determined to calm the big fella before he decided to take out his frustration on the old man, or his three companions, including myself.

Half the beer was gone, as the third round of bourbon and other drinks were set up; when the front door flew open again, once more bringing in the frigid wind and snowflakes, and a uniformed police officer! I recognized the officer as my old friend, Officer Ben Sharp. I waved him over to us. He did not have to shove his way through the crowd, as it parted for the uniformed officer as if he was Moses himself crossing the Red Sea.

"Ben, good to see you buddy, working the strip tonight I see. How's it going? Got time for a cold one?" I asked, as we shook hands.

Officer Ben ignored my offer and asked, "Is this the man whose cab was stolen?" Looking at the towering hulk as he gulped the last of his beer and nodded his head to affirm, he was the cabbie who lost his cab.

"Well, you will be glad to know your cab is parked right outside, just where you left it . . . with the keys in it, and the motor running—you idiot. Two drunk fellas left this place, saw your cab, sitting there idling at the curb, and took if for a joy ride around the block. Now I suggest you and your cab get out of here, before I write you a summons for stupidity and drinking on the job!"

The cabbie took the old man by the back of his collar and said, "Come-on old man, I am not leaving without you. The meter must be up to one hundred dollars by now, you old fool!"

As the door closed behind them, Jack, the bartender, slammed a bill on the bar, and looked at me with a glare of certainty in his eyes . . . as he barked at me—"You let that old timer leave without paying his tab, now it is yours—buddy. Pay up!"

I looked at the tab, shocked at the sudden turn of events against me. The bill for three rounds for the four of us, the old timer, myself, and my two friends, plus a beer for the cabbie, came to just under one hundred dollars. I quickly gulped down what was left of my last drink, and I told my two buddies to drink up too. I glanced toward the front door, considering a quick dash for the door, I saw in the corner of my eye that Jack yelled to someone named Parker, "Hey Parker, cover these guys."

A fella who I had not noticed was sitting at the end of the bar nearest the front door. He stood up and was clearly the tallest man in the place, and the biggest too. I saw his eyes make contact with my own, then his gaze shifted toward the rear exit, past the go-go stage, and the restrooms. I turned my head to see who he was looking at, as another fella of similar size stood up at that end of the bar and took his position by the back exit.

"Okay you two, dig out all your cash. We are not getting out of here without paying this tab, or there will be hell to pay."

My two buddies slowly shook their heads in regret. It took all we had, and I even threw in my final five-dollar bill to tip Jack, the bartender, just to not piss him off. I knew it was always a good idea to be on good terms with your favorite bartenders.

As my two buddies and I headed toward the front door, the sound of gunshots could be heard outside! The tavern door opened quickly as Officer Ben Sharp ducked inside with his pistol drawn. He yelled, "Everyone down!" Several more gunshots were heard as the wail of police sirens grew louder. I was on the floor, close to my friend, officer Sharp. "What the hell is going on Ben?" I asked.

"Those two drunk clowns who took that taxi for a joy ride around the block, just took my police cruiser around the block. They pulled up again as I got outside. One of those stupid bastards stumbled out of my cruiser and pulled a handgun. He got off one round at me and missed, before I pulled my gun and winged him. He dropped his gun. The other drunk clown took off down the alley."

There were more sirens and flashing lights, as two more police cruisers pulled up, blocking the street outside, as officer Sharp slipped back outside. The door to the tavern was ajar and I heard him shout an explanation to the arriving officers. One officer took off down the alley to chase the other "joy-riding-drunk" . . . Officer Sharp and another officer knelt over the wounded drunk who had dropped his pistol. Just then the wail of an approaching ambulance was heard.

My two buddies and I slipped out the door and moved quickly around the corner to the lot where my car was parked. We made our quick retreat, and escape, just in time, from a night we would never forget.

Once Again

Let me see you once again,
Let me hold you as before,
Then kiss your neck so softly
And kiss your lips once more—

Let me awake beside you
In the middle of the night,
And touch your hand so gentle,
To wake you not, nor give fright.

Yet, feel you touch me back,
As soft and gentle as a dove . . .
And feel again, how very much—
Yes, once again, we are so in love.

—T. L. Needham

HELENA IN DREAMLAND

IN MY DREAM, Nick, a good friend, told me he had recently opened a restaurant. I am walking along a sidewalk toward the location of the new place. It is dark and raining. Streetlights, neon signs, and car headlights are reflecting in the wet pavement. A splendid light show.

I notice in the street and parked along the curb are 1930s era cars. This tells me I am perhaps dreaming in a past life memory. I arrive at the building where my friend has opened his restaurant, an Italian place, with a narrow glass door situated on the corner. A bright red neon sign in the window reads— "NICKS".

I slide through the narrow door as someone holds it open for me. The place is fairly crowded. I walk across the room and take a table near the far corner, against the windows. I like looking outside the window at the rain, wet pavement, and the wavy reflections. I am feeling good about being here . . . my kind of place. The waiter in busy and has not even noticed me.

A young woman sits down at my table. She is wearing a pretty creamy-pearl colored dress, broad square shoulder pads, modest, and typical of this period. Her hair in a brunette bouffant, glows with a backlite color of a cherry Coke. She holds an un-lit cigarette to her lips, inviting me to give her a lite. She starts to talk to me as if she knows me, "Good to see you, handsome, again."

I listen, pulling out my Zippo, and lite her . . . then ask, "Do I know you?"

"Of course, Honey, don't you remember when we met in St. Louis? I'm Helena, the singer. You suggested I contact Nick, your friend, and the owner of this place. He gave me a job, just as you promised."

Just then, a waiter appeared and handed me a menu, without comment. I looked up, and my eyes met his empty stare. "Bring me an espresso and a Chianti," I said, as I looked at Helena, offering her a drink with my eyes, without really saying it.

Helena blows a puff of smoke, and says, "No thanks Honey, I'm working."

The waiter nodded as he turns, gave an indifferent eye-roll, and walks away.

Then Nick, dressed in a black tuxedo, came over to my table from the bar against the far wall. I had not even noticed he was there. He shook my hand and thanked me for stopping by, as he looked at Helena. "Aren't you supposed to be doing your act, or what?"

"Oh sure, whatever." Helena looked at me with a pout on her lower lip, pushed back her chair and got up, as Nick took hold of her elbow to guide her toward the end of the bar across the room. She pulled her elbow away with a haughty flip of her hair, to show me how independent she was, and to especially show Nick too.

Soft music began to play from some unseen phonograph, as Helena picked up a microphone and started singing. It was a soft, torch song . . . the kind I liked. Too bad I could not hear her over the noise of all the customers talking, and ignoring her.

I looked down at the tabletop and realized my waiter had brought the espresso and Chianti. Both were served in such a tiny cup and glass, I felt annoyed. Plus, the espresso was cold, and the wine was warm.

I looked up again to check on Helena. She had just finished her second song. No one clapped or even acknowledged her performance, if that is what you would call it. I wondered if she would return to my table. No. Nick pulled her over to the bar to join him and several noisy men he was entertaining.

I noticed the waiter was standing right beside me again. Waiting for my order, I supposed. I picked up the menu. It was all in Italian. That was okay. I had lost my appetite anyway.

The waiter ripped my check off his pad and laid it on the table and moved on. I took a glance over toward Nick to see if he might cover this one for me. He was too engaged in flirting with Helena.

I pulled a smoke out of my pocket, lit it, dropped a ten on the table to cover the check, then drained the tiny espresso, and the warm Chianti. I stood up, put on my raincoat and walked toward the door in the far corner. Just as someone opened the door for me, I glanced back at Nick, he never looked up. But Helena saw I was leaving, and she blew me a silent kiss.

That is how my dream ended, with a kiss from across a room, by a stranger I hardly knew, in another time, another era. Yet, this dream, like others—felt more like a memory than a dream. It was so real. But, how can one have a memory of something that happened in a time before you were born? Do you know what I mean?

QUINCY IS MY NAME

—⟫⟨⟪⟩⟫⟨⟪—

"I THINK IT'S time we get a new puppy. A small one, like Little Lady was," said my wife one morning. It had been about a year since our beloved little Yorkipoo had gone to Doggy-Heaven. I understood my wife's feelings.

We still had Ben-Gita, a chow mix that looked and acted exactly like Laddie, my childhood dog. Ben-Gita? Yes, I am open to the possibility that dogs, and other pets, can reincarnate, just like we humans. Why not?

"I am going out to see Dad this morning. He is expecting me. Perhaps when I get home, we can visit the animal shelters in town and find a homeless dog to adopt?"

My wife nodded her agreement, as I went out the door.

Dad and I had a nice chat, as always. As I left Dad's home, he said his usual parting request, "Call me when you get home son."

And I replied with my usual comeback, "Dad, I will call you if I do not make it home!"

"That's what I am afraid of son!"

We both chuckled as I turned and went out the door.

Driving home from Dad's place in Raytown, I decided to take the scenic route, west on 87th street to Hillcrest Road, then north into the woods of Swope Park. Traffic going in both directions was fairly heavy for this backwoods road. The ancient old trees grew right up to the two-lane road and left little or no room for a shoulder.

Suddenly I saw something in the road running straight at my truck. I came to a sudden stop. I could hear car brakes squealing behind me, as they also stopped, to avoid rear-ending me. Then the horns began to honk. No one behind me could see what I saw, or know why I stopped so suddenly.

There it was, a very small, scruffy little dog, that had run down the center of my lane, right up to me, forcing me to stop suddenly. Now I could not see the little fella. I was reluctant to move until I knew he was safe, and not in my way.

Finally, with more horns honking in protest, as the line of angry drivers behind me was growing, I saw the little fella scamper off into the woods to my right. I took my foot off the brake and hit the gas. Just then, an ambulance came towards me in the on-coming lane. The driver had his window down and was waving at me to stop [again!]. I rolled my window down as I slowed to a stop.

"Are you going to rescue that little dog?"

"Yes, if I can catch him," was my reply. Actually, I had not made that decision yet. But now I was committed.

"Good, now I don't have to rescue that little dog. Thanks!" The ambulance driver picked up speed and so did I as I looked for a spot to pull over on the shoulder. Soon, I pulled over, and came to a stop on the narrow gravel shoulder. As I set there for a moment, my voice that occasionally whispers to me from out of nowhere, said, "That ambulance driver was an angel. An Earth-Angel." Yes, I felt that angels can move among we humans on earth and guide us—or help us when we really need help.

I got out of my truck and began walking back down the road,

ignoring the glare of frustrated drivers who were behind me during my recent stop and go antics. As I walked, I searched the woods looking for the little furry fella that was so desperate to stop me, or someone, that he ran right down the middle of the road.

Now I see him. He is sitting right up against a huge tree. His silver-grey fur matches the background color of the tree bark perfectly. He was about forty feet off the road. I quietly worked my way into the woods towards him. It was cold, with patches of snow about, and the ground was damp and spongy.

As I got closer, moving very slowly, so as not to spook the little fella, I began to whisper very softly, "Here little fella, I will not hurt you . . . it will be okay."

He sat still and kept his eyes fixed on mine. I got close enough to reach out and touch him, but I held back and continued to whisper softly, as I slowly reached over to gently touch, then pat, the top of his head. He held still and seemed to accept my presence. So, I slowly slid my hand off the top of his head, down the back of his neck, to the scruff of his shoulders . . . and took a firm hold of him. He did not object, as I lifted him up into my arms. But he was shivering from the cold, and perhaps from fear too.

I took my first deep breath. I realized I had been holding my breath as I approached the little dog. Now I was so relieved, and happy too.

"Hey little fella, you look just like Toto from the Wizard of Oz. Do you know Miss Dorothy? The Scarecrow? Tinman? Cowardly Lion? No? Well, we will see about all that. You are going home with me."

As I carried the wayward dog back to my truck, I noticed I could feel his ribs. He was so thin. And his hair was thin too, with a bare belly. He was starving. Yet, he seemed relaxed in my arms, and his shivering slowed to a tremble.

Back in my truck, I took off my jacket and set it on the passenger seat to make a bed for him and help warm him up. Soon, we were out of Swope Park and I stopped at the first convenience store. I wanted to get something to feed this little fella. I came out with a hot-dog in a bun. I got back in the car and set the wiener in the bun in front of him. He sniffed it and then turned his head away. I reasoned he had never been given a hot dog before and did not know what to do with it. So, I broke it into bite size bits. Again, the little guy took a sniff, then jumped over the hot dog and leaped into my lap, with his head out my window.

At this point, with him on my lap in the warmth of the truck, I could smell this dog. He really needed a bath!

Yet, clearly, he wanted to get as far from the rejected hot dog as he could. I was shocked. I liked hot dogs. I loved chili dogs! Yet, here a starving little dog would not go near a hot dog. I wondered what he was trying to tell me about hot dog ingredients?

Soon we arrived home. My wife greeted us as we came in the door.

"Hello, what have you got there?"

She reached out to pet the little fella and to our surprise, he snapped at her!

"Maybe if you fed him, then gave him a bath, you two will bond," I suggested. "I am going to take a shower and then we can take this critter to the vet and see if he has a chip, so we can find his owner."

Later that day, we were back from the vet and had learned this little fella had no chip, no collar, no tags. He seemed to be lost, or perhaps an abandoned orphan. He was very malnourished, but otherwise healthy. The vet said he was a cairn terrier . . . just like Toto after all.

"So, I guess we should post some 'lost dog' notices around town?" I wondered to my wife.

"No. I think he was abandoned by his owners. Whoever they are, they had no tags on him, no chips implanted, and you found him in the woods far from any house or place a dog owner might live. No, someone abandoned him in the woods. We should just keep him," my wife said, with a motherly longing in her voice.

"Okay, but we should at least put an ad in the paper. Just to see if there is a lost owner out there," I suggested. My wife gave me a look that said, "Forget it, we are keeping him!"

My wife put a bowl of rice, milk and dry dog food in front of the little fella. He snarfed that down.

"Well, if we are going to keep him, we need to give him a name," my wife said.

He sat there looking at me, as I sat there looking at him. His eyes look so intelligent. It felt like he could read my thoughts. So, I said, "My goodness, you look just like Toto in the Wizard of Oz! So, is that your name, or whatever is your name? Then, the word formed in my mind, as he stared into my eyes . . . "QUINCY" . . .

"His name is QUINCY!" I exclaimed! He just told me so. And, I am pretty sure he is psychic and can communicate telepathically too! Welcome home Quincy.

Well, this story started by mentioning that we already had a dog named, "Ben-Gita." And, I felt when we adopted him at the shelter that he looked just exactly like my first puppy that I got when I was only four-years old. His name was Laddie. There never was a better dog than my Laddie. Until Ben-Gita arrived, that is. So, the question now was, how would Ben-Gita respond to having a new dog in the family?

The first test was to feed them both, at the same time, in the same room, with each having their own dog-dish. That went well. No growling or possessiveness at all. They each went to their own bowl and cleaned it up. Then, with tail wagging, looked up, as if to say, "Well, is that all there is?"

Then, I decided to see how they played together. We had a large front yard that was a perfect place for Ben-Gita and me to play fetch. I put a leash on both Ben-Gita and Quincy. Then I took them out on the front porch. I held Quincy's leash, as I un-snapped Ben-Gita's; then threw the tennis ball across the yard. Ben-Gita took off like a rocket and got to the ball before it even touched the ground! Then, as always, he playfully brought the ball back and dropped it on the ground at my feet. He stood there wagging his tail, waiting for another toss.

I looked down at Quincy to see if he was paying attention. Hard to tell actually. So, I threw the ball again, and with the same results, Ben-Gita caught the ball and instantly returned it to drop at my feet. After several more examples of proper catch behavior, I announced, "Okay, Ben-Gita, good boy, now it is Quincy's turn."

I snapped Ben-Gita back on the leash, and un-snapped Quincy's leash. I let Quincy sniff at the ball, as I explained that I would throw it, and he was to do just like Ben-Gita—catch it, bring it back, and drop it at my feet! Quincy looked at me, as his stubby tail wagged

. . . QUINCY is my name . . .

Ben-Gita, and Quincy— the ankle biter!

in expectation. So . . . I threw the ball, higher than before, to allow Quincy time to get under it for the catch. Quincy took off across the yard; arrived at the spot just in time to catch the ball in the air, and then looked back at me.

"Good boy Quincy! Now, being it back, come on!"

Without a moment's hesitation, Quincy turned his head to look away, and then took off running down the street, with the tennis ball firmly held in his mouth. Ben-Gita barked in protest!

"Well, we may never see that dog again," I muttered to Ben-Gita. As I put Quincy's leash in my pocket, and began the walk to find Quincy, with Ben-Gita beside me on his leash.

After walking several blocks, we had to pass a house we always dreaded on our usual "potty-walks" . . . A Doberman pinscher lived there. And, he was always outside, on their patio, with no fence. But he was tied with a steel cable to an anchor set in concrete in the middle of the patio. He would bark and lunge at the steel cable with a fearsome fury!

Ben-Gita always ignored the Doberman and showed him no regard or fear. Then, just as we passed the barking Doberman, I saw Quincy, hiding in the dark shadow under a pick-up truck at the curb. Again, I began my soft-whisper as I approached, still holding Ben-Gita's leash. Fortunately, Quincy stood still and let me reach in and take hold of him, then snap his leash. I tried to take the tennis ball from his month, but he was still not ready to give it up.

So, with both of my dogs now on the leash, I began our walk home, which took us past the Doberman again.

As soon as the Doberman saw us coming, he again lunged with fury and barked at us! Each time he lunged; the anchored cable

snapped him back. Until we were as close as we got to him on our re-
turn home. Suddenly, on a ferocious lunge, the concrete anchor came
loose, and the Doberman was free to charge us . . . and HE DID!

We had no time to react. Within an instant the Doberman crashed
into Ben-Gita, knocking him onto his back as the Doberman stood
a straddle over him, barking in Ben-Gita's face. I yelled, pulled, and
pushed, trying to help Ben-Gita, as both dogs ignored me. It was a
stand-off and Ben-Gita was not showing fear, but no fight in him
either. He had more of a "What's your problem?" attitude. Now the
Doberman's owner came running out of the house carrying a leash
and yelling at me to get my dog off her dog? She was looking behind
the two dogs now in combat, and as I turned my head behind me,
I saw what she was yelling about—

Little Quincy had dropped the tennis ball and was biting the
Doberman's rear leg for all he was worth. It was a three-way stand-
off. The lady grabbed her Doberman by the collar and pulled him
away, as we exchanged a few select words that suited the trauma of
the moment.

A few minutes later, Quincy, Ben-Gita, and I arrived at home.
None the worst for the encounter we had just survived. But now I
had a better idea of the nature of each of my now beloved dogs.

Ben-Gita was a loyal, loving, playful and tolerant dog. But not
a fighter, more a tolerant peace lover.

Whereas, Quincy, was a protective warrior dog, as fierce as he
was fearless. And, despite his diminutive size, he was the epitome of
the quote by Mark Twain—

*"It is not the size of the dog in the fight, but the size of the fight in
the dog."*

Wise Up

A wise person
Knows what he does not know.
Only a fool,
Believes he knows it all.

A wise person
Seeks answers to fill the void.
A fool makes them up—
Before the question is asked.

A wise person
Is humbled by their ignorance.
A fool, is arrogant . . .
Without a clue to their ignorance.

A wise person
Rarely speaks his mind.
A fool will never stop . . .
But everyone wishes he would.

—*T. L. Needham*

MISS GOINS IS GONE?

MY EARS WERE numb from the machine-gun like explosions of the strings of firecrackers. We had been setting them off in the dark for over an hour at the corner crossroads, where our gang gathered for this event. The racket and flash of the exploding fireworks was always a thrill. The fact that the fireworks were illegal added to the delight. None of us could afford, nor were we allowed to have fireworks. Except Leslie, an only child, whose folks always bought him a big mail-order box of fireworks. Yet, Leslie being the youngest and smallest in our gang always allowed Charlie, my older brother, and his pal Vern, to set off the fireworks for us younger boys. They would have done so anyway, because no one could stop them.

"Leslie, you come home now," came a shout from up the street. "I have to go home, Mom's calling me, must be bedtime," Leslie said. He and I really enjoyed watching fireworks go off. But we both wished we could set them off ourselves.

As Leslie stood to walk up the block to his house, I heard him say with a sudden rush of fear, "What is that . . .?" I stood up quickly and turned around. We were standing on the darkest corner of the intersection, the side without a streetlight overhead. He was gazing at the house on the corner, pointing his finger, with his jaw drooped open.

It was an old house, just like all the big homes in this neighborhood. But the weird thing about this house was that there were no lights on at all. Only total darkness inside the house. Except, "Look there . . ." Leslie whispered, with a fearful tone in his voice that made me shudder. Then I saw what he was seeing, what he was pointing at, what made him so frightened.

Each window on the front of the house was totally black. There was not a single light on in the entire house, except one tiny eerie red glow right in the middle of the picture window on the first floor. You could barely see it. Then, as I strained my eyes to focus on and understand what this tiny red glow was, it expanded for an instant and suddenly grew brighter, and then subsided back to its normal glow, it seemed to breathe. It was alive!

I looked at Leslie in amazement. Something in the dark old house was alive and sitting there in total darkness, just watching us out that window. "I'm going home." Leslie whispered, as he took off running down the block. I looked back at the light. It still just glowed but did not breathe brighter again.

"What's going on?" Charlie asked, as he and Vern walked up behind me. I realized now that all the other kids had gone home. It was getting late, and bedtime had already passed. I said nothing, not wanting to show my fear like Leslie, so Vern and Charlie would not torment me, or make fun of me for being a coward. I turned around and pointed at the dark old house with the blacked-out windows, and the strange eerie glow of a small red light in the middle of the picture window. In that instant, as all three of us peered at this tiny red glowing light—it breathed bright again! This made it seem so alive . . . and that was very unnerving.

"That must be old lady Goins, just sitting there in the darkness, smoking a cigar. That's all," said Vern, sounding confident in his explanation.

"Are you sure?" Charlie asked. "Why are there no lights on in that house? And how come we've never seen anyone come or go from that old house? I've never even heard of 'old lady Goins!'"

"I have never seen her either. No one has as far as I know. She is very old and has lived in that house longer than anyone who lives around here can remember. But she is blind and smokes cigars. That's what my dad says, and he knows all about her because he works at the grocery store where she has her food delivered to the house once each week," Vern explained, proud of himself for having information no one else had.

Another flare-up on the red glowing light as it seemed to breathe again. "Let's go knock on her door and see what happens!" Charlie said, with mischievous glee in his voice.

"Won't do any good. She is deaf too," Vern added.

"Bull! You're making all this up," Charlie said, giving Vern a punch on the shoulder.

"Charlie! You boys come home—NOW!"

"That's Mom calling us Charlie, we better get home," I said, as I took off running home and putting distance between me and that creepy old "Goins house." Within a few minutes I was snug in my bed, under the covers, sound asleep, and off to dreamland.

The next morning as I set off on my walk to school, I looked around and no other kids were in sight. Maybe I was early, or late—whatever, but I kept going. I got down to the corner; the one we would now call "Goins' Corner," and thought about the creepy old lady named "Goins." Her house did not look so creepy in broad daylight. Then I noticed that the front door was standing wide open. There was a black funeral hearse parked at the curb. I stopped and stared into the open door. I could see two men picking up something, no, someone—covered with a large white sheet and place them on a gurney. Then they began to roll the gurney with the sheet-covered body out the front door, onto the porch, and down the sidewalk toward the waiting hearse parked at the curb.

"Who is that?" I asked, feeling more than a little creepy again.

"Sonny, this is Miss Goins. She passed away last night. Poor old thing was over 100-years old too. Deaf and blind all her life. Grocery delivery boy found her first thing this morning, sitting in her rocking chair right there in front of that big picture window," one of the men explained as they loaded the shrouded remains of old Miss Goins into the hearse. "Yep, old Miss Goins is gone," he said, as he slammed the back door of the hearse.

As I walked to summer school, my dream about Miss Goins buzzed in my mind. I spent the entire day thinking about poor old Miss Goins. Sitting there in the darkness, which for her was never ending, in silence—an eternal silence now, I guess. I wondered so many things. How did she manage? What would it be like to not see or hear anything? It must be a lot like being dead all the time. I guess that does not make sense. And did she really die? She could not see or hear what we were doing last night in front of her house—our noisy fireworks war zone. Unless some how she felt it, all the loud bursts, exploding fast. Maybe we upset her. I could not get her out of my mind.

Later that night, after it was dark and everyone had gone to bed, and the neighborhood was quiet. I found the courage to get up, get dressed and sneak out of the house. Some strange curiosity compelled me to go out of my house, my own safe home, and walk down the street to "old Miss Goins' house."

I do not really know why. It was like I was summoned, compelled, or beckoned to come in the darkness again to the creepy old house of this strangely afflicted and mysterious old lady. Finally, I reached her front gate. I stood there looking at the dark old house with all the windows blacked-out, and no light coming from within at all.

Then I drew my eyes to the big picture window. Nothing. Not like last night. No eerie, red, breathing glow. I do not know what I expected, but I felt a gentle release of my fear, a reassurance that all was right, and good, and okay, just as it should be . . . then it happened! The red glow—IT WAS STILL THERE! It seemed as if old Miss Goins was sitting with her back to the window and had just turned around toward the window and took a big draw on her cigar. It breathed glowing bright red again, just as the night before, then back down to the steady glow. I felt goose bumps rise on my arms and could feel the hair on the back of my neck standing straight up, and my heart was pounding as my body shivered with a frightful chill.

How can this be? What can this be, making this strange eerie red glowing light? Miss Goins is gone—she is dead. They said so, in my dream. I saw them take her away . . . didn't I?

I ran home as fast as my feet would move me. I quietly slipped back into my house, up the stairs and climbed into my own bed; where I slept the rest of the night with my blanket over my head, again, and my bedroom door closed and latched! Because, with that old Miss Goins' house . . . I saw more in my dreams . . . than when I was awake!

No Escape

There is no right,
There is no wrong,
So, no matter how
You sing your song,
Your good intentions
May be too bad to mention.
But they are only actions
To provoke reactions,
Falling fast in sequence
Is the consequence . . .
You'll never escape—
The hearts you break!

—*T. L. Needham*

THE CISTERN

YOU MIGHT THINK I am mad, insane, or just crazy; or something like that. But I am not mad, or crazy, or insane. I am only four years old. I am still trying to find my mind in this senseless world—not lose it.

But I am curious. And I am fearless. These two traits do make many people think I am also crazy.

We just moved into a house that is over 100 years old. My Dad and Mom love this house. It is so much nicer than the old house we rented that backed up to the steel mill. I liked that house. I liked to look out the back screened door at night and watch the wonderful sparks fly as the steel was being made and shaped into wonderful steel things.

The lights would flash, and sparks would fly, and noises were heard that you could never imagine. I loved the view from the back door at the old house.

But Mom and Dad said it was too noisy, and it smelled bad too. So, they bought this lovely 100-year old cottage that overlooked Turkey Creek. Our new home had a front porch and a bigger back porch, two bedrooms, an indoor toilet and bathtub. We all really thought that was a big improvement! But Dad said the house had no basement. Only a small root cellar and a crawl space. He said he would like it more if it had a full basement. For me, the small cellar and crawl space seemed to be the most interesting part of the house. My intense curiosity had been awakened.

The entrance to the cellar was a big door on the back porch that you had to lift up and swing to one side, so it leaned against the house. I watched Dad open the cellar door not long after we moved in. He went down a steep stairway as I watched him disappear into the darkness below. The darkness was so complete, so black in its total nothingness, that I worried Dad would just be swallowed up in this black pit. I yelled out, "Dad!" No answer. "DAD!"

"What!" came back an irritated answer. "Where are you Daddy?" I asked anxiously. "I am in the damn cellar, where else? And you get the hell back from that cellar door!" My Dad was a man of few words, unless he was angry; then most of his words were curse words. I was learning fast.

I did not step back as Dad demanded. I saw the beam of his flashlight circle about in the darkness, and from this I knew he was still alive and the voice I heard was his and not some devil demon.

I was a Catholic child and had not yet gone to school to learn about life from the nuns. But my older brother and sister had been to school already. They always talked about school a lot and what they were learning, especially about the devil. So, I knew all about the devil, who lived in the dark place under ground; just like our cellar.

Dad was down there in the cellar for a long time. So, I did not step back as Dad demanded. But no one else was around to help Dad if he needed it. So, I just sat there on the top step of the stairway to the cellar, looking down into the darkness below.

Later that evening at dinner, Dad started talking about his trip into the darkness he called a cellar. "Just an old dirt root cellar." He said to Mom. "Dirt floor, no stone walls even, and a shallow crawl space just barely big enough to crawl around in. But I did find an old cistern to catch water near the corner of the crawl space."

"Dad, what is a cistern?" the curious part of me asked without even thinking. That is the problem with being curious; it is spontaneous and rarely ever gives any thought to the consequences. I heard someone say that once. Maybe it was my Mom.

"Son, a cistern is a way of catching rainwater in the old houses. They would dig a deep pit under the house, line it with stone, just like a deep well, and then route all the gutters on the house to run all the rainwater directly into the pit. Then a pump would be set in the pit and they could pump the water right into the house. Almost as good as running water like we have in the house today. Do you understand, son?"

"No." I answered. "So, Dad, there is a deep pit under our house?" I asked, still trying to complete the picture in my mind. Dad said yes there was. And then I asked a question that could have changed the course of my personal history. "Dad, where is the cistern— the big, deep pit under our house?"

"Son, as near as I can tell, it is directly under your bedroom. Maybe right under your bed."

That did it. Now he had fully inflamed the curious mind within me. I began to imagine that just under the floor of my bed was a deep, black, bottomless pit. Perhaps it went all the way to hell itself!

"Dad, what's in the cistern pit? Is it full of water now, or what?" I wondered out loud.

"Son, it may have water in it, I cannot be certain. I could barely move myself when I found it and did not care what was in it. I do not want you to even think about this. Just forget about it, okay?"

"Honey, what *is* in the cistern-pit, don't you really know?" Mom asked Dad with more than a little worry in her voice.

"It could have been full of water, or maybe just a few feet or more, or after all these years it is actually dry and just full of dead air." Dad answered Mom.

"Dad, what is dead air?" I asked, before Mom could ask the same question.

"That would be air at the bottom of a pit that is heavy, stale air, no real oxygen, nothing to breath. If you fell into a hole or that cistern, you would most likely suffocate before you would drown!" Dad said, getting tired of the questions.

"How do you know the air is dead Honey?" Mom asked Dad, pleading for more information.

"Well, my Dad, Grampa to you—," as Dad shot me a sharp look to insure I respected what he was going to say, "—said to lower a kerosene lantern into the cistern pit to see what's at the bottom, and how deep it goes. But, also if the light in the lantern goes out before it gets to the bottom, then the air is dead, and no one would survive if they went into that cistern." Dad said.

"What did you find when you did this?" Mom continued to probe.

"The lantern went out after only about six feet, so the cistern is nearly full of dead air. I dropped several rocks down into the darkness and I did not hear any splash. So, I think it is dry and maybe about ten to twelve feet straight down," Dad said, as he took another bite of his dinner and washed it down with a gulp of coffee.

"So, what are you going to do about this, dear?" Mom asked Dad.

"I am going to dig out that cellar and put new stone walls under the short walls we have now. As I dig, I will throw all the dirt I dig out into the cistern pit until I fill it up. Then I will put a permanent cap on that cistern, so it is sealed and safe. Then I will pour a new concrete floor over the dirt floor of the big cellar and we will have a nice, new basement." Dad answered with some irritation, still chewing on his roast beef.

"Dad, will you show me the cistern pit some time?" I asked.

"No son," Dad said, very irritated to make me understand he was tired of all the questions and not wanting to encourage my growing curiosity. "As I said before, you stay the hell out of the basement and forget all about that damn cistern!" His anger had reached the point that he was pointing his finger at me and his eyes got so big, I knew this was the end of the discussion about the cistern. Dad always meant what he said, especially when he pointed his finger right at you, and got so angry one of his eyes was squeezed nearly closed.

The next day was Saturday. My Dad was off work and planned to work in the cellar all day. The first thing he was going to do was install a light in the basement so he could see what he was doing. He then installed a switch for that light on the back porch near the stairway to the cellar, so he could turn off the light as he came and went into the cellar. Dad was very good at planning things like this and he could do anything.

I stayed close by and kept an eye on what Dad was doing. But I just played with my toy race cars in the dirt and did not bother

Dad. He would make me go inside and play if I bothered him. So, I did not, for sure.

After a little while, Dad came out of the basement and walked across the back porch to the kitchen door. He told Mom, who was working in the kitchen, that he needed a few things and was going to the hardware store. Then as Dad walked down the back porch steps and rounded the corner toward his car parked in the driveway near the front sidewalk—he shot a quick glance at me, and had that look in his eyes that said, "You stay out of trouble, or else . . ."

As I watched Dad's back, he walked up the driveway, got in his car, started it, and backed out of the gravel driveway into the street, then drove off down the street. My eyes moved over to the back porch, Mom was in the kitchen busy working on dinner, no other kids were around, just me—and then my eyes moved over to the cellar doorway. Dad had left the door open to the cellar. I could never lift that door by myself. No one was around. No one would know if I went into that basement to check out this cistern myself. No one would know. I could not get in trouble if no one knew.

I walked up the steps onto the back porch, looked at Mom through the screen door, she was busy and did not even notice me. Then I turned and slowly walked over to the wide-open cellar door and peered down the steep steps into the dark cellar below. Only now, the cellar was not so dark, because Dad had left the one little light bulb still on in the basement. As I began the decent into the cellar, I took one last look at the light switch on the wall near the cellar door. No one was around, surely no one would turn off that switch, surely not.

I began to back down the steps, one by one. They were too steep for me to walk down them any other way, and there was no handrail to hold onto. As I backed down the steps, I could not actually see where I was going. Each step backwards only took me further down into the dimly lit cellar. And, the cellar door opening above me got smaller and smaller, with less light, and less blue sky to see above me.

Finally, my foot touched the dirt floor. I was now at the bottom of the stairway. For a moment, I hesitated, putting my other foot on the ground too. A moment of doubt, or even fear, ran through my mind. "Do I really want to do this?" I silently asked myself. If Dad finds out I will really be in trouble. He seems to worry all the time that I will do something stupid and get hurt. Then I thought about my guardian angel. Everyone has one. My older brother and sister told me all about this, after the nuns at school told them. I said a short, silent prayer, to my guardian angel to protect me, as I put my other foot firmly on the ground.

I slowly turned around and took in my surroundings. One lonely light bulb now hung in the center of the ceiling of the cellar. Then only dark dirt walls on all sides and a dirt floor. The cellar was small. I could walk from one wall across to the other with in eight or ten steps. But to my right, just a few steps away, was my Dads' step ladder leaning up against the dirt cellar wall. I knew this ladder was how my Dad got up to the crawl space and found the cistern.

"Perfect!" I said to myself. I had not even thought about how I would get up into the crawl space to investigate the cistern. But my Dad had taken care of that for me by leaving the ladder against the wall, just where it needed to be to help me up. I slowly walked over to the ladder. It was dark even with the small light bulb. I was worried about bugs. I hated bugs and did not want to step on one, or have a spider drop down on me. For a moment, as I considered where I was going and my dread of spiders, I thought maybe I should just go back up the stairway to the blue sky and well-lit back porch.

No. My intense curiosity ruled me at this point. It compelled me to continue up the ladder and find the cistern. I just had to know, I had to understand what this was all about. I climbed up the step ladder to the top. Only about six steps. Then, as I reached the top and peered into the crawl space, I realized the one lonely light bulb hung lower on its cord than the level of the dirt floor crawl space. This low hanging light bulb now cast a shadow across the crawl space dirt floor, leaving it in total darkness. But I was committed now and began to crawl arm over arm as I pulled myself along the dirt floor. I was beginning to feel claustrophobic too. No room to stand or even rise up to my knees. The crawl space only allowed me to lift my head a little as it touched the floor joists above.

But, after crawling about the length of my own body, with each reach and pull forward, arm over arm . . . my next arm forward reach did not touch the earthen floor of the crawl space! Instead it just dropped straight down into empty black space. I had reached the edge of the cistern! And, my head, arm and shoulder were now hanging directly over the black, empty void of nothingness called the "cistern."

A rush of panic filled my mind and my heart began to pound. I realized I was within inches of falling forward over the edge of the cistern. A fall that would result in certain death from suffocation, if the fall into the black pit of darkness did not kill me first. I decided it was time to get out of there—NOW! I reached back with my left hand down to my side and dug my fingers into the dirt. I pulled with all my might to shove myself backward from the edge of the pit. But I realized the pulling was actually dragging my body forward, further over the edge of the cistern edge . . . I was nearer to the point of losing my balance and falling headfirst into the dark cistern. My right arm was useless as it hung over the edge of the cistern, and there was nothing I could take hold of—nothing, but black, empty space.

My dire and helpless state rose into absolute panic when at that very moment I heard footsteps over head on the back porch . . . it was my Dad! I could tell by the heavy tread of his steps. Help was on the way. But no! Instead I heard the cellar door slam shut and in the next instant the light in the crawl space went out! Dad had turned out my only source of light . . . I now had no idea which way was backwards or forwards—if I could move myself from the edge of the cistern. But I did hear a low muted voice say, "Hi Honey, is dinner ready?" Dad asked my Mom in the kitchen above the cellar. I realized in that instant that if I could hear them maybe they could hear me . . . HEELLLPPPP!" I yelled as loud as I could. But, with my head hanging over the cistern, my cry for help went straight down into the pitch-black empty darkness below. I turned my head to the side to try and project my voice up, out of the black pit of death below. "HELP!" I cried in one burst as loud as I could manage. Even that effort, the rise and fall of my chest to make this big yell for help, seemed to inch me even closer to the edge, and the fall into the black pit that already seemed to be my certain fate.

There were footsteps on the back porch above! The light just came back on in the cellar! I heard someone coming down the steps into the cellar— "Damn! Where the hell are you?" I heard my Dad say, and in an instant, I felt the grip of his strong hands on my ankles and with a none-too gentle jerk, pulled me by my ankles back from the edge of the death pit called the . . . "cistern".

Before I could take a breath to exhale the dust from my lungs, Dad had me on my feet on the cellar floor. He brushed dust off me as he asked, "Are you OK son? What on earth are you doing down here?"

I could not even summon an answer from my panicked brain. Dad scooped me up in his arms and rushed us both up the cellar stairs, into the fresh air on the back porch.

Dad sat down on the steps of the back porch, still holding me in his arms. Mom came rushing out the back door of the kitchen with a worried look on her face that broke my heart to know how much I had scared her too.

"Son, what on earth were you doing down there?" Dad asked with a worried, panicked look on his face.

"I just wanted to see the cistern Dad." I whimpered.

"Well son, I hope you got a good look, because you are never going into the cellar again! Do you hear me?" Dad said, in his firm, I really mean it, voice.

Mom took over from there and walked me into the house and then to the bathroom. She began to draw bath water and peeled off my dirty clothes. "No dinner for you until we clean you up." she said.

I heard a noise coming from the back porch and stood on my tip toes to look out the window. Dad was already installing a pad lock on the cellar door.

Later that night, I laid in bed in the darkness, with the moonlight glowing through the sheer curtains of my one-bedroom window. I thought again about the deep black cistern in the crawl space, just below the floor where my bed was sitting . . . and I knew it still wanted me, beckoned me—

"Come to me, it said . . . I will take you to another world and another time . . ."

I turned over on my side and covered my head with my pillow, and silently said to myself, "NO. I like it here just fine."

Farewell—22.11.1963 . . .

On a cold, November day . . . a shot is heard!
Then another, and another . . . from the grassy knoll?
A misty fog is gathering across the land . . .
It is becoming very hard to see . . .
Hours of waiting, then a voice on the radio says—
"The Spirit has left the body."
Rivers of tears begin to flow across the earth,
As hope for a better world just left the planet.
Camelot is now closed—forever.
Who could do such a thing?
Even the Angels are asking, "Why . . .?"
The torch is passed to a new generation. Again.
But all too soon—for we are not yet ready . . .
To say, "Farewell."

—T. L. Needham

THE RING

AN ACHING BEGAN to creep into his joints, as he bounced along in the wagon, heading for his homestead. The late afternoon sun was shining in his eyes, adding to his growing discomfort. But weary as he was, he knew he could fall sound asleep and his horse pulling the wagon would deliver him safely to his homestead, only a few miles southwest of Shelbyville.

As they plodded along the old Vandalia stage road, Curtis Bayard Needham gradually became aware that he was not only weary, he was becoming gravely ill too. And that very thought filled his heart with dread.

After spending the morning digging graves to help bury the many friends and family members who had once again fallen victim to the dreaded cholera, he looked forward to returning home to his beloved Margaret, and their two children. His mind could not help but dwell on so many graves that had pushed out the boundary of the Shelbyville cemetery in the past year, due to this terrible plague.

Why, only last summer, nearly one-third of the residents of the county fell ill and died within just a few miserably hot months. Including his own elderly mother and father. So many people fled the county to escape the cholera that gravediggers became scarce. The few able-bodied men who could dig worked day and night to kept up with the demand of the new resting places for the unfortunates.

Yet, the dead still waited in silent rows of coffins for days in the summer heat, until their final resting place was made ready.

Only a few had fallen to cholera this summer. But today, August 29th, 1856, was destined to be a day that would affect the future generations of this family for the next hundred and fifty years. For as Curtis rode on, he became increasingly feverish, and eventually fainted across the wagon seat. Dutifully, the horse did deliver him up to the lane to his home, and family.

Margaret Needham was anxiously awaiting her husband's arrival. She worried constantly about the dreaded illness that struck down so many members of her family and community. Less than a year ago, her own nine-month-old daughter, Eliza Jane, was taken by cholera. But life on the Illinois frontier kept her plenty busy with other matters of survival. She and Curtis still had their two children, John, seven years old, and Lydia, only four years of age. They would make a warm and loving welcome for their father when he arrived. She had made his favorites for dinner and knew he would be exhausted and perhaps depressed after this long day. At last she heard the familiar plodding of the horse's hoofs coming up the lane to their home. Margaret called to the children, "Dad is home, come and greet him!"

When Margaret reached the doorway, her heart nearly stopped. For there was the horse pulling the wagon up the lane to the house, but Curtis, her husband, was not sitting erect in the seat holding the reins; as she had seen him do countless times before.

Margaret ran out to stop the horse and rushed to the front of the wagon only to find Curtis unconscious and slumped down across the seat.

John was close behind and asked in an anxious voice, "What's wrong with Dad? Why isn't he moving?"

Lydia stood in the doorway, holding her corncob dolly, and sensing something very bad was happening, but she could not know, or understand her mother's dreadful concern.

Margaret did not answer John, but in her heart, she feared that she knew the answer all too well. She told John to unharness the horse from the wagon and lead it to the barn and tend to its needs. Then she climbed into the wagon and took Curtis's arm over her shoulder. Frontier life had made her strong and what she lacked in size she made-up with inner strength. Somehow, she got Curtis into the farmhouse and into their bed. He was feverish . . . his color a pale ashen pallor. He had all the symptoms of cholera, which she had come to know only too well.

Curtis died before midnight. If there was anything merciful about cholera, it was sudden, lethal, and quick.

Margaret did not sleep that night. She set up beside her husband, who now lay still and silent in their bed. She closed his eyes and washed him. Dressed him in his only suit. Kissed his cool lips one last time.

As the faint glow of dawn began on the eastern horizon, Margaret stood in the doorway of the house. Facing east, the doorway caught a cool early morning breeze, and it provided some meager relief from the heat, but nothing could relieve the terrible grief she felt from this sudden loss; or stop the pain from the tight lump in her throat.

Yet, deep within her, she knew she felt the first stir of new life. She had suspected for weeks that she was pregnant, but hesitated to mention it to her husband, Curtis, until she was certain. Now it was too late to tell him. Too late to see the joy in his eyes when he heard the news. For Curtis was a loving man who enjoyed and loved his family, especially his children.

Margaret also thought about her unborn child. This child who would never know its father. She said a silent prayer to herself that she may live long enough to have this baby, and God willing, raise all her children. Then she vowed to herself, in the early glow of dawn, with the sun just beginning to light her face, that if this child was a son, he would have his father's name, Curtis, in loving memory of the father he would never know.

Curtis Bayard Needham II was born February 6, 1857, only six months after the death of his father, Curtis Bayard Needham.

I do not know what actually happened to Curtis Bayard Needham. All I am certain of is that he died on that summer day, August 29, 1856. I do not know how he died. Nor do I know where he died. I do not even know where he is buried. But, my years of research have provided me with clues, and someday I hope to find his final resting place. Lacking this information, I can only imagine, based on my research on the life and times of the Illinois frontier of the mid-19th century. What you have just read is my fictitious notion of what might have happened nearly 150 years ago.

Curtis Bayard Needham is my great, great, grandfather. He

never knew his son Curtis Bayard Needham II—due to his untimely death before his son was born. His son, Curtis Bayard Needham II, was the father of my grandfather, Charles Vernon Needham, who fathered my dad, Charles Vernon Needham, Junior.

However, this is not the end of the story of my great, great grandfather. No, for me, it is actually the beginning of a quest that began early in my own life, when I was just a boy. For reasons I cannot explain, I have always felt a great need to know more about my Needham family history. There were few shreds of information available, most of which proved to be inaccurate, and nothing factual and definitive was revealed. For example, whenever I asked my grandfather, Charles Vernon Needham, senior, about our family history, he would advise me to, "Never shake the family tree; you never know what might fall out." I suspect that is exactly what he had been told all his life. And his father, Curtis Bayard Needham II, was most likely told the same thing, given that he was raised as a stepson in the Duckett household.

Even less help came from my own father, Charles Vernon Needham, Junior, when I asked him about our Needham family history. Dad always said we were "Black-Irish" . . . but he could never explain what that meant or provide further details. Being stubborn and determined, a family trait that took deep root within my nature, I endeavored to research the origins of "Black-Irish" to reveal a murky history for the term. I learned that at various stages "Black-Irish" was almost certainly used as an insult. However, the label of "Black-Irish" seemed to emerge in recent times as a point of honor among certain Irish descendants or immigrants. The exact origin of the term is vague and most likely had a number of different origins. It seems to be a descriptive term, rather than a reference to an actual group of Irish people. Thus, I was left to wonder where my own dad got the idea we were "Black-Irish" in the first place.

I never had the opportunity to know my great grandfather, Curtis Bayard Needham II, because he died in 1936, and I was born in 1944. However, I did know his wife, my great grandmother Ida [Phillips] Needham. She was a vibrant and happy spirit, who always had a flower pined to her dress, and a pleasant smile, plus the sunny disposition to go with it. She died in 1959, when I was fifteen years old. Just a few years later my father decided to pass on to me several items that he obtained from her estate. Dad gave me the only tools left behind by great grandfather Curtis, who was a carpenter and homebuilder, all his life. The tools included a weathered old wooden level, with all the finish worn off, and one brass-butt plate missing on the end. The other tool was an old worn square. There were others Dad could have passed these items on to, yet he chose me, and I treasured them beyond words.

Then, a few years later, when I was 18 years old, Dad gave me an old Cowboy Ranger .38 caliber six-gun, with a walnut grip, covered with a thin layer of rust. This pistol was a reproduction of the famous Colt revolver carried by most cowboys. Dad told me the old revolver was found in a sea-trunk under a false bottom at Granny Ida Needhams home when she died. It was missing the hammer mechanism. But, to me, it was another treasured relic of my ancestors. I carefully restored the old pistol and had a new hammer made by a friend.

Dad also gave me an old brass Yankee drill that belonged to my great grandpa Curtis. It was an1896 Goodell-Pratt Automatic Drill, with eight fluted-shank drill points stored in the handle; and a rotating indexed cap that released one drill point at a time; equipped with a split two-jaw chuck; and brass body. This was a fine and handy drill for any carpenter to own, and my great grandpa would have been about 40 years old when he acquired this tool, right in his prime.

As time went by, I was compelled to collect old wood working tools. Carpenter work seemed to be in my nature, as well as home building. So, by the time I was thirty years old, I was also a home-builder. Over the decade of the 1970s I built over 50 custom homes.

About 45 years ago, in the mid-1970s, my restlessness with this uncertainty finally reached the point of intolerance. I began a serious and determined mission to research my Needham family history. In my travels I visited local libraries and searched their genealogy records for any "Needham" records. If I found anything, I would write letters to local genealogists, asking for more details. All this was long before the internet.

I had no idea what I was getting into. As the years passed, I made little progress. I found many Needham records and traced the names all the way back to the earliest settlers of this land from England. But for many years, I was unable to connect my "lost-branch" of descendants from Curtis Bayard Needham to any other Needham family line. This includes the very prominent Needham families who pioneered central Illinois in the early 19th Century.

Then in December 1985, a breakthrough occurred. A letter arrived from a fellow genealogy researcher, Opal Soetaert, that urged me to focus my research on the Needhams of central Illinois in Effingham County.

Opal suggested that my Needham family line is connected to the Needham Pioneer Cemetery located north of Rosemont, Illinois. This connection could tie in our branch of the Needham family to those Needhams.

A few weeks after Ms. Soetaert's letter arrived, in mid-January, I made a business trip to Chicago. On the way home, I planned to do some research on my family history. I arrived at Shelbyville by noon. It is a charming and historic old town on the edge of a great lake. As I drove around, I found the cemetery, and as I always did, walked past each tombstone seeking Curtis Needham, or any Needham. No luck.

Then I went to the library and while it was a charming small library, I found no records that could help me in my quest. However, the librarian suggested I visit the Shelby County Historical Society. She was certain they would have helpful records. Alas, as I arrived at their headquarters, I found they were closed. I would have to try again.

Sitting in my car, trying to decide what to do next, I considered seeing if I could find the Needham Pioneer Cemetery. I reasoned it must be south and east of my present location, and perhaps about 20 miles, more or less. As I considered this idea, happy snowflakes the size of nickels began swirling about . . . each seemed to be a joyful spirit beckoning me to follow them. I put the car in gear and headed south on a gravel road right out of town.

As I drove along, the old farmhouses and barns all seemed ancient. The only sign of modern times were the power/phone lines along the road suspended on thin poles. Soon I came to a wooded area as the gravel lane descended into a creek basin. This wooded area seemed so familiar to me . . . I felt I could remember hunting here as a young man. Yet, how could that be? I have never been here before . . . not in this lifetime.

Driving along the rural gravel road, I came to a "T" crossroad. I could not continue straight ahead, but had to choose, right or left? As I sat there trying to decide, I felt . . . or heard . . . a chorus of voices in my head saying, "Turn left!" Then, next time, "Turn Right!" Seven times I came to such a crossroad and each time, the chorus in my mind provided an answer. I had a growing feeling that my car was full of happy spirits of my Needham ancestors, and we were heading for a "coming home party" very soon.

After a few more crossroads and turns directed by my spirit family in the car, I came to a bend in the lane as the road became sheltered by a thick stand of brambles and thickets on both sides. Suddenly, in my peripheral vision I registered the name— "NEEDHAM"! I came to a sudden stop as my tires slid in the gravel. I backed up as I looked intently to my left. There, I saw, . . . about 20 feet off the road, nestled among tall cedar trees, was a tombstone, with the weathered and hardly legible name—NEEDHAM.

I sat in my car for a moment, feeling complete amazement. I realized the happy spirit voices, after seven times telling me the right way to turn at each crossroad, had brought me exactly to my objective. So, what are the odds of that? The odds are one chance in 128 times. This was not a lucky coincidence.

I got out of the car and climbed across the ditch along the road and found a way through the brambles. There I was, with nickel size snowflakes swirling about me, staring at a tombstone, among many, that read—Daniel Parkman Needham. The tombstone was so weathered it was very hard to read, except on this day; those happy-nickel size snowflakes had stuck in the grooves of every word on that tombstone, outlining them in white and making the words perfectly readable. Another amazing coincidence, or was it?

I walked about in the blowing snow and considered each stone. There were mostly Needhams, with a few other names included. The largest stones were for Daniel Parkman Needham, then his wife, Juliana. Next was the tombstone of Daniel's father and mother, Elias and Elizabeth Needham. Alas, I did not find a tombstone of my great, great grandfather—Curtis Bayard Needham. My quest continues.

It was getting colder, and light was fading, plus I was hungry. So, I returned to my car and soon found I-70 highway. I headed west toward Effingham to find a room and a meal. After checking in, and eating dinner, I found the Effingham Library and was directed to the genealogy room. There, I found a treasure trove of information on the generation of my Needham pioneer ancestors who moved into Cumberland County Illinois.

While researching various records I finally found the link of my great, great grandfather, Curtis Bayard Needham, to his parents, Elias (b. 1780) and Elizabeth (Gibbs) Needham. Their children included:

*Gravestone of
Daniel Parkman Needham.*

*Gravestone of Juliana—
wife of Daniel P. Needham.*

b. 1802-- Elias Wells Needham

b. 1804 – Daniel Parkman Needham

b. 1806 – Rachel Ann Edson [born Needham]

b. 1808 – Laura Gibbs [born Needham]

b. 1810 – Angeline Gibbs [born Needham]

b. 1812 – William B. Needham

b. 1818 – Ann Edson [born Needham]

b. 1822 – Curtis Bayard Needham

b. 1827 – Mary Anne Beals [born Needham]

The first thing I learned about his generation of Needham pioneers in central Illinois was their friendship and interactions with Mr. Tom Lincoln, and his now famous son, Abraham:

Abraham Lincoln, by name Honest Abe, was a rail-splitter, river-raft man, champion wrestler and more, in this youth. All before he became the Great Emancipator and lead the nation through the Civil War. (born February 12, 1809) near Hodgenville, Kentucky, U.S.—died April 15, 1865.

CUMBERLAND COUNTY ILLINOIS HISTORY:

10.25.2017 - [from website]

Lincoln, Needham, Gibbs – 1832

Posted on May 14, 2015

In 1843 part of Coles County was organized as Cumberland County. Elias Needham and his son, Daniel Parkman Needham, took an active part in organizing Cumberland County. Elias

Needham served as an election judge in the Woodbury precinct that year. Partial list of the children of Elias and Elizabeth Needham: Elias Wells Needham; Daniel Parkman Needham, b. August 18, 1804; Rachel Ann Needham (Mrs. Daniel Edson); Laura, Angeline, and William B. Needham.

Several of Rachel Edson's Needham cousins lived around Neoga, Illinois. A cousin, Elias Parkman Needham of New York City, brought forth the reed organ, invented the up-right action and originated the idea of a perforated sheet passing over a reed chamber and held fifteen patents, there-on. (Ref. Who's Who in America)

The Edsons and Needhams soon after arriving in Illinois became acquainted with the Gibbs family, one of the very first to settle in Coles County. The following year the Abraham Lincoln family settled nearby. Rachel Edson's brother, Daniel Parkman Needham, Elijah Elias Gibbs, and Abraham Lincoln became firm friends and did many things together.

Elijah Elias Gibbs, on February 7, 1832, married Angeline Needham, (sister of Daniel Parkman Needham, as well as Curtis Bayard Needham) and sister of Rachel Edson. Their first home was in the Springfield, Illinois area. Abraham Lincoln helped Gibbs in splitting the rails which fenced the Gibbs property. Elijah and Angeline (Needham) Gibbs attended the wedding of Abraham Lincoln and Mary Todd.

One of the well-remembered events of those days was the trip down the river to St Louis on a raft loaded with pelts. Daniel Needham, Elijah Elias Gibbs, and Abraham Lincoln built a raft and made the journey after a successful winter of trapping.

Laura Needham, Rachel Edson's sister, was being courted by Abraham Lincoln. This courtship, lasted several months or until Elijah Elias Gibb's brother, Homer, appeared. (Note, Elijah and Homer Gibbs are kin to Laura and Rachel's mother— Elizabeth Gibbs-Needham.) Homer Gibbs: "cut Lincoln out" and married Laura on July 18, 1833. Some of the Needham family said Mr. Lincoln and Laura were engaged, others said they had talked of marriage. Laura and Homer Gibbs lived in Sullivan and in Mattoon, Illinois. She died near the close of the Civil War and he immigrated to Missouri.

Daniel Needham and his friend, Abraham Lincoln, were both husky men and they often wrestled. The Needham men were six footers, weighing around two hundred pounds. All were outstanding members of their communities.

Daniel Needham purchased land (Section Sixteen), south of Daniel Edson's home place in Coles County, Illinois, from Abraham Lincoln's father, Tom. There is a Lincoln marker on the property. Needham served as Justice of the Peace in 1839 and 1859. He took a leading part in organizing Cumberland County in 1843 and in 1844 he was a County Commissioner candidate.

Later he moved to Effingham County and settled two and three quarters miles northwest of Montrose. He was a large landowner. He was buried in the Needham Pioneer Cemetery diagonal to and across the road from his home (d. February 16, 1876, age 71 yrs., 5 mo., 28 days). He and his wife Julia A. were born in Penn.

Then, I found this in:
Following in Lincoln's Footsteps—by Ralph Gary:

> *Daniel Needham challenged Abraham Lincoln to wrestle at Paradise Post Office at Wabash Point (about one-mile due west of Exit 184 off I-57) and due east of the southern end of Lake Paradise. Lincoln was five years younger, than Daniel, but more than a match for any man.*
>
> *Tom Lincoln, (Abe's father) bought, then sold to Daniel Needham "PLUMMER PLACE," about a half-mile due south on the west side of 900E, and half mile north of County Road 100N, where Tom Lincoln lived for a short time in 1837. Then Tom Lincoln moved on to Gooseneck Prairie, where he lived until 1840. His son, Abe, visited many times (16 in fact).*
>
> *Elijah Elias Gibbs was one of the first families to settle in Coles County Illinois in 1825. He became a large landowner. His son, Rev. Elijah Elias Gibbs was a close friend of Abraham Lincoln and they did many things together. One spring, after a successful season of trapping, Gibbs, Abraham Lincoln, and Daniel Parkman Needham built a raft and took the furs down the river to the market in St. Louis. Their experiences on this trip were retold many times.*
>
> *Rev. Elijah Elias Gibbs told his daughter that Daniel Parkman Needham threw Abraham Lincoln at a wrestling match.*

Continuing the story of this interesting generation of Needhams I find in the writings of Abraham Lincoln's long-time law partner, and

first biographer, William H. Herndon, in the Lincoln Biography—
LIFE OF LINCOLN, page 64:

*In June the entire party, including Offut, boarded a steam-
boat going up the river. At St Louis they disembarked, Offut re-
maining on foot. At Edwardsville they separated, Hanks going
to Springfield, while Lincoln and his step-brother followed the
road to Coles County, to which point, old Thomas Lincoln had
meanwhile removed were Abe did not tarry long, probably not
over a month, but long enough to dispose most effectually of one
Daniel Needham, a famous wrestler who had challenged the
returned boatman to a test of strength. The contest took place at
a locality known as "Wabash Point." Abe threw his antagonists
with comparative ease, and thereby demonstrated such marked
strength and agility as to render him forever popular with the
boys of that neighborhood.*

In yet another version of this same incident Richard Kigel wrote
in his book: THE FRONTIER YEARS OF ABE LINCOLN (IN
THE WORDS OF HIS FAMILY AND FRIENDS) page 124-125,
published in 1986:

*When the boys had enough of New Orleans they headed
for home, Offut, Johnston, Abe and myself (Dennis Hanks) left
New Orleans in June 1831, Hanks recalled. "We came to St.
Louis on the steamboat together, walked to Edwardsville, twen-
ty-five miles east of St. Louis—Abe, Johnston, and myself. Offut
stayed behind in St. Louis. Abe and Johnston went to Coles*

County and I to Springfield, Sangamon County. Tom Lincoln had moved to Coles County in 1831, I say June."

Abe went home again to help his father with yet another move. He didn't remain long, probably just over a month. While he was there, he heard a loud, good-natured challenge. The undisputed champion wrestler in the county was a giant named Dan Needham. The champ had been hearing all about the new tall boy over at Goose Nest. "I can fling him three best out of four any day," he boasted.

There was a house-raising at Wabash Point and a big crowd was there. Abe and Big Dan Needham eyed each other, and a war of nerves was on. The two giants stood face to face, each six foot four, each a mountain of muscle. "Abe," said Tom Lincoln, "rassle him."

They set upon a ring and the crowd egged them on. Four times Needham went down. The last time, Big Dan Needham lost his head and came at Abe fists flying. Abe calmed him down with this friendly manner and finally Needham offered Abe his hand. "Well I'll be damned," he said.

. . . Abe was now twenty-two years old. He was the wrestling champion of Coles County, Illinois. He had conquered the Mississippi and been down to New Orleans twice. He was a farm hand, a butcher, a boatman, a carpenter, a merchant and a clever speech maker He was his own man. Abraham Lincoln was ready to take on the world.

"It must 'a ben about that time 'at Abe left home for good," said Dennis Hanks.

Daniel Parkman Needham's youngest brother, and also my great, great grandfather, Curtis Bayard Needham, would have been 9-years old in 1831—when these events occurred. Odds are pretty strong he witnessed these events, along with his Dad and the rest of the Needham family.

It was getting late as I researched what I could find in the Effingham library. I was very pleased and excited to learn so much about my great, great grandfather and his family in the Illinois frontier days of the early 19th Century. Then I decided to take a few more minutes to see what I could find on Curtis Bayard Needham himself. I was not disappointed. I found a deed to land acquired by Curtis and his wife, located in Rose Township of Shelby County, Illinois.

I had studied the PUBLIC LAND SURVEY SYSTEM in college. Plus, my career had included years in real estate brokerage, development, and home building. So, if I had a legal description, I could find the property. I printed a copy of the Township map for Shelby County, and the road map too. I felt it would be interesting to at least see the land they owned, and perhaps where my great, great, grandfather lived and farmed. And, especially where he died; and his son, my great grandfather, Curtis Bayard Needham II was born, after his father's death.

With a determined resolve and anticipation, I set out that next morning from Effingham back to Shelbyville, where my quest had started the day before. I felt the same presence of happy spirits with me, urging me on with a sense of excitement that now, at long last, the lost Needham clan of my ancestors would be reunited.

Once again, as I turned off the main highway, and headed west, then turned to the south, along a wooded gravel road; I felt a sense of time reversing . . . going back to days when my family lived in this area. Soon, I came to the tract of land that should be my family's, back in the early 1850s. From right to left, it was level plowed ground, good, rich, black crop soil. About 100 yards to the west the field was lined by a dense wood. A creek flowed in the trees. It was scenic country.

Then, as I slowly drove along on the gravel road, in a misty fog, I saw an old farmhouse in a clearing in the woods. There was a gravel lane from the road to the house that had seen little or no wear and nearly overgrown. Still, I felt beckoned by my spirit companions to have a closer look. I picked up my camera, turned off my motor, and got out of my car. I looked to see if anyone was about that might resent my trespassing, Or, perhaps I could ask permission to see the old house. In the cold, early morning mist, with no one was around, and the nearest house a mile down the road. I decided to listen to my inner voice that urged me to walk down the grassy lane to the house.

As I approached, I could see the weathered silver-grey home was a clapboard sided, two story dwelling. The paint had long since weathered away, and the roof still had many of the original green shingles. The home was surrounded by tall trees and overlooked a wide creek bed behind the house. I was impressed by the details that showed a flourish of pride in the ornamentation of trim and brackets. The home implied a sense of dignified grandeur, without being pretentious. I stepped inside. I felt like I was back in time to the 1850s. There was no evidence of a single modern improvement. No wiring. No inside plumbing. It seemed as if time was frozen here

. . . the home had not been occupied for a very, very long time. Yet, in spite of the weathered old walls, glassless windows, sagging floors, and cracked plaster . . . *it felt like home to me.*

Curtis Bayard Needham homestead.

Curtis Bayard Needham homestead, window details.

After my own father's death in 2010, I was given the last item that belonged to my great grandfather, Curtis Bayard Needham II. My sister, Skye, found a ring in our father's desk. It was a platinum signet ring with gold initials— "CN". The ring fit me perfectly, like a long-lost puzzle piece needed to complete a picture. I treasured this relic from my Needham ancestor, and I have not taken it off once since I put it on my finger ten years ago.

For as a ring is a circle, this ring seemed to close the circle on my quest to be united with my ancestors . . . *my family.*

One of the most interesting things about life is death. The end of "life"—or is it? Then there is birth, the beginning of life . . . or is it? Or, is life and death only two sides of the same door? We pass into life from one side . . . the spirit world, and back upon our death . . . to the spirit world? I believe we are spiritual beings, who live human lives from time to time. And, while we are in the human world, our spirit friends and family, in constant contact, guide us along the path we are destined to follow. If only we learn to listen to their whispered guidance and follow that guidance wherever it may lead us on our mission of discovery.

I cannot explain my life-long determined commitment to unravel the story of Curtis Bayard Needham's life. I do not know how, or why, we are connected. But I do know this . . . *we are connected.*

And, not only do I believe I am connected to my great grandfather, and while I do feel a special and strong connection that drove me to research and discover my lost family history and connections to others. I have also learned that each of us are a link in a chain of uninterrupted life going back to the beginning of human existence. While we think of ourselves as a single individual who was born, and in time, will die, we are much more than this. We are a link in the chain of life, that goes on and on. That chain of life goes back in time and doubles with each generation, in that you have two parents, four grandparents, eight great grandparents . . . and going back just twenty generations . . . we each have 1,042,176 great grandparents!

It seems to me that if we have thousands of ancestors, and if reincarnation is a fact, it also seems a certain number of past-life memories may also be retained, from one life into another. Perhaps even in our DNA, somehow, memories survive, to be recalled in another time, another life. So much of what I have described herein felt more like it was driven by long-lost memories of loved ones, from another place, another life, another time.

Clearly, as we go back in time, there were fewer people and therefore, the greater number of "family-connections" we share . . . thus—*we are all connected.*

During my years of research, I have found the graves of many of my ancestors. Yet, I have never found the grave of my great, great grandfather, Curtis Bayard Needham. I suspect he was buried in a mass grave, along with the many other victims of the terrible cholera epidemic at that time. So, while I never found his grave, I still ask myself, why was this so important to me? Perhaps, I just wanted to say hello. Or, perhaps goodbye. Or, just to say, I am here again . . . and you are not forgotten . . . and now you will be remembered—*always.*

Curtis Bayard Needham II –
my great-grandfather, ca. 1900.

⟫⟫⟫ ⟪⟪⟪

There are many accounts of the wrestling match between Abraham Lincoln and Daniel Parkman Needham. There are variations in the conversation and challenges between the two men. However, each offers colorful insights into the times, and customs. Thus, they are included below:

EARLY ACCOUNTS OF LINCOLN'S WRESTLING MATCH WITH DANIEL NEEDHAM [google]

Wayne Whipple's Account:

Sometime in June the party took passage on a steamboat going up the river, and remained together until they reached St. Louis, where Offutt left them, and Abe, Hanks and Johnston started on foot for the interior of Illinois. At Edwardsville, twenty-five miles out, Hanks took the road to Springfield, and Abe and Johnston took that to Coles County, where Tom Lincoln had moved since Abraham's departure from home. Scarcely had Abe reached Coles County, and begun to think what next to turn his hand to, when he received a visit from a famous wrestler, one Daniel Needham, who regarded him as a growing rival, and had a fancy to try him a fall or two. He considered himself "the best man" in the county, and the report of Abe's achievements filled his big breast with envious pains. His greeting was friendly and hearty, but his challenge was rough and peremptory. Abe met him by public appointment in the "green-wood" at Wabash Point, where he threw Needham twice with such ease that the latter's pride was more hurt than his body.

"Lincoln," said he, "you have thrown me twice, but you can't whip me."

"Needham," replied Abe, "are you satisfied that I can throw you? If you are not, and must be convinced through a thrashing, I will do that, too, for your sake."

Needham surrendered with such grace as he could command.

The Story Life of Abraham Lincoln: A Biography Composed of Five Hundred True Stories Told by Abraham Lincoln and His Friends, Philadelphia: The J.C. Winston Company, 1908, pages 84-85.

W. M. Thayer's Account:

A few days after Abraham reached his father's house in Cole's County, a famous wrestler, by the name of Daniel Needham, called to see him. Needham had heard of Abraham's great strength, and that he was an expert wrestler, and he desired to see him.

"S'pose we try a hug," suggested Needham.

"No doubt you can throw me," answered Abraham. "You are in practice, and I am not."

"Then you'll not try it?" continued Needham.

"Not much sport in being laid on my back," was Abraham's evasive answer.

"It remains to be seen who will lay on his back," suggested Needham. "S'pose you make the trial."

By persistent urging Abraham finally consented to meet Needham, at a specified place and time, according to the custom that prevailed. Abraham was true to his promise, met the bully, and threw him twice with no great difficulty. Needham was both disappointed and chagrined. His pride was greatly humbled, and his wrath was not a little exercised.

"You have thrown me twice, Lincoln, but you can't whip me," he said.

"I don't want to whip you, whether I can or not," Abraham replied magnanimously; "and I don't want to get whipped;" and the closing sentence was spoken jocosely.

The Pioneer Boy, and How He Became President: The Story of the Life of Abraham Lincoln, London: Hodder and Stoughton, 1882, page 164.

William O. Stoddard's Account:

This second experience of river life in the South left the young giant little better off than before in worldly goods, whatever else he may have gained by it. But while he was away his talkative friends had taken good care of his reputation as a man of muscle. They had said so much, indeed, that the champion wrestler of that region, one Daniel Needham, sent him a challenge to a public trial of strength and skill. It was accepted, as a matter of course, and the meeting took place with all the customary prairie formalities; but rarely has a "champion" been more astonished than was Daniel Needham. It was not so much that he was thrown twice in quick succession, but that the thing was done for him with so much apparent ease; and his wrath rose hotly to the fighting point.

"Lincoln," he shouted, "you've thrown me twice, but you can't whip me."

"Needham," said Abe, "are you satisfied I can throw you? Well, if you ain't, and I've got to satisfy you by thrashing you, I'll do that too, for your own good."

The crowd laughed, but the champion gave the matter a sober second thought, and concluded that his own good did not require a mauling from that man. He was entirely satisfied already.

Abraham Lincoln: The True Story of a Great Life, Showing the Inner Growth, Special Training, and Peculiar Fitness of the Man for His Work, New York: Fords, Howard, and Hulbert, 1885, page 72.

Charles Godfrey Leland's Account:

He had hardly returned, before he received a challenge from a famous wrestler, named Daniel Needham. There was a great assembly at Wabash Point, to witness the match, where Needham was thrown with so much ease that his pride was more hurt than his body.

Leland, *Abraham Lincoln and the Abolition of Slavery in the United States*, New York: J.P. Putnam's Sons, 1881, page 33.

L. NEEDHAM

Ward H. Lamon's Account:

Scarcely had Abe reached Coles County, and begun to think what next to turn his hand to, when he received a visit from a famous wrestler, one Daniel Needham, who regarded him as a growing rival, and had a fancy to try him a fall or two. He considered himself "the best man" in the country, and the report of Abe's achievements filled his big breast with envious pains. His greeting was friendly and hearty, but his challenge was rough and peremptory. Abe valued his popularity among "the boys" too highly to decline it, and met him by public appointment in the "greenwood," at Wabash Point, where he threw him twice with so much ease that Needham's pride was more hurt than his body.

"Lincoln," said he, "you have thrown me twice, but you can't whip me."—

"Needham," replied Abe, "are you satisfied that I can throw you? If you are not, and must be convinced through a thrashing, I will do that, too, for your sake."

Needham had hoped that the youngster would shrink from the extremity of a fight with the acknowledged "bully of the patch;" but finding him willing, and at the same time magnanimously inclined to whip him solely for his own good, he concluded that a bloody nose and a black eye would be the reverse of soothing to his feelings, and therefore surrendered the field with such grace as he could command.

WORKS CITED:

The Life of Abraham Lincoln from His Birth to His Inauguration as President, Boston: James R. Osgood and Company, 1872, pages 84-85.
Daniel Edson Story. Soetaert, Opal Miller.
Bethany, Mo., "BB" Engraving and Print. Co., 1969
CUMBERLAND COUNTY ILLINOIS HISTORY:
10.25.2017 - [from website]
Lincoln, Needham, Gibbs – 1832
Posted on May 14, 2015

Following in Lincoln's Footsteps: A Complete Annotated Reference to Hundreds of Historical Sites Visited by Abraham Lincoln (Illinois)
Paperback – November 22, 2002
by Ralph Gary (Author)
Paperback: 498 pages
Publisher: Basic Books; Reprint edition (November 22, 2002)

Herndon's Lincoln: The True Story of a Great Life
Paperback – March 6, 2014
by William Herndon (Author)
Paperback: 258 pages
Publisher: CreateSpace Independent Publishing Platform (March 6, 2014)

THE FRONTIER YEARS OF ABE LINCOLN (IN THE WORDS OF HIS FAMILY AND FRIENDS)
By Richard Kigel-page 124-125, published in 1986.

Self-Doubt—

Writing feels like digging a ditch.
You take shovel in hand,
Bend over, shove blade hard into dirt.
Your back begins to ache,
Sweat breaks out on your brow,
And, you could really use a drink, as
Self-doubt whispers in your ear,
Until the shovel is full of words,
Pitched over your shoulder into a pile.
The pile of words slowly grows,
But the ditch seems to go on forever . . .
And you wonder if it will ever end . . .
And, Hell, does the world really need . . .
One more ditch—or another pile of words?
I hope so, because I have more stories to tell.

—*T. L. Needham*

IN APPRECIATION:

MY GREATEST LEVEL of appreciation goes to the following, without whose tireless role in this project, it may never have been written.

Theresa (Needham) Green, my editor deluxe, who is also a career educator, the first-born grandchild of her generation to my parents, and my niece. Her devoted editing has made my writing far better than I could ever do without her.

And, Patty-Skye Needham, my sister, who provides the greatest continued level of support, encouragement, and endless source of memories of our lifetime we have shared.

And, foremost in my heart, Nona Jo Fowler, my cheerful muse, tireless reader/editor, supportive-critic, and darling wife.

Last, but not the least, I am grateful to Don Brent, of Don Brent Photography, Topeka, Kansas, for granting a copyright release to reproduce the picture of: *The Little Flower Girl*—Angela Marie Noelle Needham, my dear daughter.

A final word of appreciation, from my heart, goes to all my friends, fans, and family, who have read my other books, and encouraged me to continue to tell my stories. This book is also dedicated to you, and would not exist without your support. *Read on dear ones!*

T. L. Needham – Books & Awards:

WHEN I WAS A CHILD
Gold Medal – Global eBook Awards
Bronze Medal – Readers Favorite
Finalist – USA Book News Best Books Awards
Honorable Mention – Best Cover, Global eBook Awards
Honorable Mention – Writers Digest Self-Published Awards

KITTY CLAUS
Gold Medal Winner – Readers Favorite

PESKY POEMS
Silver Medal Winner – Readers Favorite

THE SHE WOLF
Honorable Mention – Readers Favorite

My books may be ordered from any bookstore, or:
Outskirts Press: https://outskirtspress.com/wheniwasachild
Amazon: https://www.amazon.com/author/tlneedham
Website: http://tlneedham.com/

Also by
T. L. NEEDHAM

When I Was
A Child

On Ash Wednesday, 1926, a young couple, Alex and Theresa, left their six children home on the farm. They drove through heavy rains to attend Mass in town. That's when the temperature dropped fast, and the heavy rain became a snowy windswept blizzard.

Only one of them would survive that night.

The terrible loss upended the lives of this working-class family in ways no one could have expected. Through it all, the ironclad bonds of love held them together as they endured the Great Depression and an unceasing string of trials, losses, and hardships.

Based on actual events, When I Was a Child documents the inner strength, courage, and sheer grit that steadied the couple's children through loss, economic crises, tornados, dust storms and war. Focusing on the extraordinary life of Louis Pfeifer, this vividly rendered book juxtaposes vignettes of a tragic past—the loss of a mother, father, and grandmother—against Louis's harrowing experiences as an 82nd Airborne paratrooper and prisoner of war during World War II. What emerges is an inspirational story of love and family bonds as Louis and his siblings grow up to become devoted, successful parents—despite all odds.

Powerful, honest, and unflinching, When I Was a Child is about the suffering that life inflicts—and the bravery that gets us to the other side, becoming much wiser and stronger along the way.

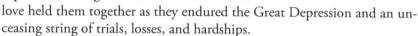
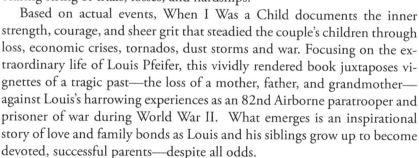

Learn more at:
www.outskirtspress.com/wheniwasachild

═══ *Also by* ═══
T. L. NEEDHAM

The She Wolf

When 14-year-old Teddy Bredwell's dog Chase takes off after a she-wolf in the woods, Teddy fears his beloved pet is gone forever. Despite his parents' warnings not to venture into the woods alone, Teddy sets out to find his dog—but what he discovers in the shadows of the thick trees is a world beyond this realm and reality. There is a time, just after sundown, when the full moon rises in direct opposition to the setting sun. A time before the sunlight surrenders to the darkness…and the full moon's glow asserts its will against the dark…and the sky is no longer blue, but not yet black… and hovers in an electric glow of deep indigo. But only on the most rare of nights, the night of the Blue Moon, the Indigo Blue Moon. During this time, deep in the woods, there is a realm where we are no longer here… we are there. We can find ourselves in a space between day and night, between light and dark, between today and tomorrow…between this realm and another. And, perhaps in that time, and that place, we will come upon those who are not from here…but from there.

Learn more at:
www.outskirtspress.com/theshewolf

Lightning Source UK Ltd.
Milton Keynes UK
UKHW051829100620
364748UK00001B/12